I N V E S T I G A Ç Ã O

IMPRENSA DA
UNIVERSIDADE
DE COIMBRA
COIMBRA UNIVERSITY PRESS

EDIÇÃO

Imprensa da Universidade de Coimbra
Email: imprensa@uc.pt
URL: http//www.uc.pt/imprensa_uc
Vendas online: http://livrariadaimprensa.uc.pt

COORDENAÇÃO EDITORIAL

Imprensa da Universidade de Coimbra

CONCEÇÃO GRÁFICA

Imprensa da Universidade de Coimbra

IMAGEM DA CAPA

by Jonathan Velasquez via Unsplash

INFOGRAFIA

João Emanuel Diogo

PRINT BY

KDP

ISBN

978-989-26-2276-7

ISBN DIGITAL

978-989-26-2277-4

DOI

https://doi.org/10.14195/978-989-26-2277-4

DEPÓSITO LEGAL

504476/22

OBRA PUBLICADA COM O APOIO DE

COSTA, Hermes Augusto

ILO-Chair at FEUC : talks on the
future of work. - (Investigação)

ISBN 978-989-26-2276-7 (ed. impressa)

ISBN 978-989-26-2277-4 (ed. eletrónica)

CDU   331

HERMES AUGUSTO COSTA

EDITOR

THE "ILO CHAIR" AT FEUC

TALKS ON THE FUTURE OF WORK

SUMÁRIO

Hermes Augusto Costa[1]

This book brings together texts by experts from the International Labour Organization (ILO), followed by commentaries provided by professors of the Faculty of Economics of the University of Coimbra (FEUC) who are also, in most cases, researchers at the Centre for Social Studies (CES) or at the Centre for Business and Economics Research (CeBER).

The idea behind the book: celebrating the ILO Chair

In order to talk about the "ILO Chair" and how it came to be hosted at FEUC, we need to trace the important steps that led to its creation: first, the conferral, in 2009, by the University of Coimbra (UC), following a proposal from its Faculty of Economics, of the degree of Doctor Honoris Causa on the then Director-General of the ILO, Juan Somavia; next, the signing in 2010 of a protocol between the UC (represented by CES) and ILO's International Institute for Labour Studies, aimed at fostering the exchange of research results

---

[1] University of Coimbra, Faculty of Economics, Centre for Social Studies.

https://doi.org/10.14195/978-989-26-2277-4_0

on employment and labour relations and promoting student mobility; most important of all, however, was the event (jointly organised by the ILO's Lisbon office, CES and FEUC) held at FEUC during the academic year 2016/2017: the simulation of an International Labour Conference. This was the first event of its kind ever to take place at a European institution of higher education. As part of the simulation, UC students were invited to discuss the "future of work" (the central theme chosen to mark the ILO's centenary in 2019). This proved to be an extremely enriching pedagogical initiative.

Thus, the creation of the ILO Chair, in the 2nd semester of the 2017/2018 academic year, was the culmination of a process of growing institutional interaction that brought FEUC's faculty and student body into closer contact with ILO specialists. Under the terms of the UC-ILO Agreement, every year the ILO Chair hosts technical staff with expertise in key ILO topics, with the aim of promoting the sharing of knowledge in areas of common interest. Also provided for in the Agreement is the exchange, between the two institutions, of documents, studies carried out by them, research results, best practices, etc. The present book is, without question, one of the most important fruits of the ILO Chair.

Until 2022, there have been five editions of the ILO Chair at FEUC. This book is a compilation of the contributions of the first three – covering the years 2018, 2019 and 2020 –, but in fact it goes beyond that time frame. What this means in practice is that the crucial issue of the pandemic is inevitably mentioned in a number of chapters as well as in most of the commentaries on them.

The dynamics of teaching and research

The goals of the inter-institutional cooperation pursued in the framework of the ILO Chair are a multifarious and interconnected

expression of the dynamics of teaching and research. As far as teaching is concerned, the dynamism and wide diversity that characterise
the ILO Chair are a direct reflection of the various courses offered at
FEUC: 4 first degrees, 12 Masters programmes, 14 Doctoral programmes and 8 postgraduate courses. Attended by nearly 3,000 students,
FEUC has 4 major disciplinary areas – corresponding to degrees in
Economics, Sociology, Management and International Relations – that
can claim a rich history and account for about 60 percent of the
courses taught. Other relevant areas and focuses of teaching are law,
history, mathematics, and scientific management methods. Both at
the first degree level and at the level of postgraduate studies (which
account for about 40 percent of the teaching carried out at FEUC),
these areas are a constant stimulus and a source of debate for themes
that are highly relevant to and convergent with the ILO's own issues
and concerns. FEUC being a multidisciplinary Faculty makes it possible to envision the future of work from a variety of complementary
perspectives. An apposite illustration of such a convergence with the
ILO's strategic goals and agenda is the doctoral programme in the
area of Sociology, entitled *Labour Relations, Social Inequalities and
Trade Unionism*, created in 2008/09, also as a product of a FEUC-
CES partnership. The programme in question aims to equip students
with innovative theoretical tools and an in-depth analysis of social
inequalities, labour issues, and the challenges currently facing the
labour and trade union fields.

As for the dynamics of research, they are clearly visible in the work
carried out at CES and CeBER. Since 1978, CES' research team has
engaged in inclusive, innovative and reflective research on Portuguese
society from a comparative, international and interdisciplinary perspective, in which special attention is paid to the "Global South" and
the expression of critical, citizen science. It is not surprising that work
and labour relations are on the long list of research topics explored
at CES, notably since, in 2022, they were given pride of place as part

of two of the Centre's thematic lines: *(Semi)peripheral Capitalism: Crises and Alternatives*, and *Democracy, Justice and Human Rights*. The more recently created CeBER (2016), centred primarily around two of FEUC's key areas (Economics and Management), has geared its activities towards such domains as innovation and organisational development, institutions and policies for sustainable development, and health policies, among others.

Themes and methodology

The themes covered in this book are both topical and extremely relevant. As mentioned above, they correspond to a selection of the contents of the seminars held in the first three editions of the ILO Chair. Thus, the book analyses and comments on four different themes. The first is *ILO's historical legacy and its contribution to decent work*. It amounts to a crucial historical assessment of the century--long role played by the ILO and, at the same time, an invitation to identify the most important moments in the life of the Organisation. The notion of "decent work" is revisited in this context and its future developments are weighed within the framework of multilateralism and the 2030 Agenda for Sustainable Development.

The second theme revolves around *labour standards, jobs and climate challenges*. An analysis is offered of the impacts of the relationships between workers, companies and trade policies and due consideration is given to the potential of labour arrangements in the framework of trade agreements. In this context, there seems to be no doubt that political guidelines are increasingly necessary if we are to make the transition to environmentally sustainable economies leading to more and better jobs.

The third theme has to do with *inequalities, work, and the gender gaps*. On the basis of facts and figures, the authors address this issue in terms of income inequality, its recent trends, and the key role of labour markets in this entire process, and also to seek explanations for, and to move towards a better understanding of the persistence of the gender pay gaps.

Finally, the fourth theme – also of great relevance in these times – focuses on the interconnections between work, *the digital economy, and the right to disconnect.* As a result of the technological innovation processes that are shaping, more and more profoundly, today's new working environments and conditions, it is imperative that we have a clear picture of the place currently occupied by digital labour platforms, as well as a good grasp of their main features and of the challenges faced by those whose work is based on them. Furthermore, by becoming a frequent (and often forced) option for a number of sectors of the economy during the pandemic, and given its propensity to blur the boundaries between work and non-work, telework has rekindled the debate on the "right to disconnect".

The specific content of these themes (or thematic clusters) was substantively expanded by the ILO experts, who were invited to write a chapter based on their participation in the sessions of the first three editions of the ILO Chair. Then, to complement these contributions, a number of FEUC professors and/or researchers from FEUC's main research centers (CES and CeBER) were challenged to write (as co-authors) a commentary on each chapter. The outcome is this conversation held with the ILO on the future of work, based on the various disciplinary perspectives that make up the FEUC community (and sometimes through comments whose authors come from very different scientific fields). Thus, the expertise of the authors of the chapters is further enriched by that of the commentators.

It is also important to point out that the chapters of the book were written at different times. While it is true that some date from before the pandemic (and therefore the written versions of the public seminars on which they are based reflect the specific circumstances of the moment in which they were held), it is no less true that their authors did not fail to address the pandemic crisis and its impacts whenever they felt it pertinent to do so. The crisis brought about by the pandemic has greatly highlighted the need to place labour centre stage, to insist on its worth and to stress the importance of strengthening the various forms of solidarity and collective identity.

The book structure

The book is divided into four parts, corresponding to the thematic concerns described above. In part I – *The ILO between the historical legacy and the future of decent work* –, chapter 1 (by Dorothea Hoehtker) is a celebration of the ILO's centenary and of its key role with regard to negotiation in a changing world. Hoehtker's essay is commented on by two historians from FEUC, Álvaro Garrido and António Amaro, who establish a dialogue with the author by locating Portugal vis-à-vis ILO's own history. Chapter 2 (by Kirsten-Maria Schapira-Felderhoff), devoted to the relationship between decent work and multilateralism, is commented on by sociologists Marina Henriques and António Casimiro Ferreira, who take as their point of reference the notion of decent work and the transconstitutionalism of social inclusion as promoted by the ILO.

Chapter 3 (by Christian Viegelahn), in part II – *Labour standards, jobs and climate challenges* –, discusses the relationship between trade, employment and labour standards, with commentators Susana Garrido and André Saramago contributing a perspective that combines the fields of management and international relations while exploring the relationship between work and social responsibility in a post--COVID world. Chapter 4 (by Guillermo Montt) argues in favour of the creation of robust legal frameworks aimed at promoting decent work and environmental sustainability. The chapter is commented on by economists Luís Cruz and Eduardo Barata, who stress the way in which jobs depend on a number of environmental economic functions.

In part III – *Inequalities, work and gender gaps* –, chapter 5 (by Patrick Belser and Khalid Maman Waziri) emphasises the need to take urgent and effective actions in the labour market with a view to reducing inequalities. The same goal is advanced by the two economists (Luís Moura Ramos and Margarida Antunes) responsible for the corresponding commentary, who in fact go beyond primary distribution of income to consider other aspects pertaining to the functioning of the labour market. Chapter 6 (by Catarina Braga) analyses the ILO Global Wage Report and seeks to explain the gender pay gaps. This analysis is commented on by two sociologists (Virgínia Ferreira and Mónica Lopes) who provide additional explanations for such asymmetries and offer different approaches while seeking to combine the ILO's methodology with Portugal's specific circumstances.

Chapter 7 (by Uma Rani), included in part IV – *Work, digital economy and the right to disconnect* –, is about the significance, characteristics and typologies of digital labour platforms, which can be the source both of multiple opportunities and challenges for workers. Elísio Estanque and Dora Fonseca's sociological commentary on Rani's chapter shows a concern with the need to preserve the dignity of those who work in the platform economy, calling for alternative and more inclusive paths. Finally, chapter 8 (by Jon Messenger) examines the evolution of telework in a context in which workers are frequently pressured to be available for work at all times no matter where. The commentary on this last chapter is by Catarina Frade and Tiago Santos Pereira. Combining legal with science and technology studies perspectives, the two authors warn, *inter alia*, against the reproduction of inequalities and the regulation of tensions that are inherent in teleworking, while pointing to some of the trends that can be observed in the European context.

Although each of the book's parts can be discussed separately, the connections between them and between their underlying themes are very clear. This becomes especially evident in the book's concluding section, the purpose of which is not to wrap up debate or attempt a summary of the various contributions (both chapters and commentaries). On the contrary, it consists of an effort by Manuel Carvalho da Silva – a former union leader and the current coordinator of CES-Lisbon and of the Collaborative Laboratory for Labour, Employment and Social Protection (CoLABOR) – aimed at exploring new avenues of reflection based on his expertise on the dynamics of the world of work. In addition to highlighting some aspects linked to the establishment of the ILO Chair, the author stresses the importance of ILO's tripartism and dwells on some of the high points of its century-old history. He also emphasises the Organisation's contribution to the social contract, a notion which, according to him, needs to be revived as we are faced with the uncertainties and inequalities exacerbated by the pandemic and new challenges are being posed by the digital world with regard to the future of work.

Let me add a couple of observations by way of conclusion. The first, which has already been hinted at, has to do with the present book's inter-thematic and interdisciplinary nature, which makes it possible to recommend it to a wide and diverse readership. It is a useful book for ordinary citizens wishing to get better acquainted with the problems currently facing the world of work as well as the major trends and the challenges ahead. However, it is aimed at other important readers beyond this general audience: university students (from various levels); teachers and researchers, both Portuguese and non-Portuguese, with an interest in topics related to the world of work and its future; social partners (representatives of employers and workers' associations); public officials and technical staff (especially those associated with the Ministry of Labour, Solidarity and Social Security or with any of the Ministry's services and offices); etc.

Finally, a word of thanks. First and foremost, to all the authors of the contributions in this book, be they the ILO specialists responsible for the book's chapters or the FEUC professors and the researchers from CES and CeBER who responded with their commentaries. By doing this, they have increased the visibility of the ILO Chair and helped strengthen the inter-institutional social dialogue and the sense of identity and community that is necessary if we are to advance our thinking and our actions regarding the future of work. A no less emphatic thank you goes to the team at the ILO's Lisbon office, headed by Mafalda Troncho, with special mention going to Fernando Sousa Jr. and Mariana Trigo Pereira, with whom I have worked in the organisation of the various editions of the ILO Chair.

References

Costa, Hermes Augusto (2017a), "Debating the future of work: a trail-blazing simulation of an ILO International Labour Conference at the University of Coimbra", *Transfer – European Review of Labour and Research*, 23 (4), 503-507.

Costa, Hermes Augusto (2017b), *O futuro do trabalho em debate: simulação da Conferência Internacional do Trabalho na Universidade de Coimbra*. Coimbra: Imprensa da Universidade de Coimbra.

(Página deixada propositadamente em branco)

I

THE ILO BETWEEN THE HISTORICAL LEGACY AND THE FUTURE OF DECENT WORK

CHAPTER 1:

100 YEARS OF ILO:

NEGOTIATING WORK IN A CHANGING WORLD[1]

Dorothea Hoehtker[2]

1. Introduction

The Centenary of the ILO was an occasion to look back at its long history and highlight the considerable amount of research which has been carried out in the past decades. After the first comprehensive studies, following the ILO's 50th anniversary[3], historians in the early 2000s became more interested in transnational labour history and particularly in the ILO. The tripartite structure proved to be a unique lens through which labour issues and labour policies could be studied in an international perspective. In the run-up to the Centenary, the number of studies from different angles and disciplines increased significantly.[4] The ILO's Century

---

[1] This paper was received in May 2020 and corresponds to the participation in the seminar "ILO History" (1st edition of "Cátedra OIT/ILO Chair"), held at the University of Coimbra, Faculty of Economics (FEUC), on February 22, 2018.

[2] Historian and senior researcher at the ILO Research Department.

[3] Alcock, A. (1971) History of the International Labour Organization (New York, NY: Octagon Books); Ghebali, V.-Y. (1989) The International Labour Organization: a case study on the evolution of U.N. specialised agencies (Dordrecht: Martinus Nijhoff).

[4] Rodgers, G., Lee, E., Swepston, L. and Van Daele, J. (2009) *The Quest for Social Justice, 1919-2009* (Geneva: ILO); Kott, S.; Droux, J. (eds) (2013) *Globalizing Social*

https://doi.org/10.14195/978-989-26-2277-4_1

Project gathered insider knowledge and strengthened the exchange with the academic community.[5] The rich and diverse research, which has not only analysed the achievements of the ILO, but also its problems and setbacks, is the basis for the following historical overview. It describes how the ILO reacted to the rapid changes in the political and social-economic context and how it has adapted its activities while maintaining its constitutional mandate of social justice and peace.

2. From the beginnings of international labour law to the creation of the ILO

With the creation of the ILO in 1919, the idea of regulating industrial capitalism through international labour law found for the first time its expression in a permanent institution. The ILO was and is a unique organisation, because it brings together the most important actors of the world of work: employers, workers[6] and governments.

However, the roots of international labour law go back to the beginning of the 19th century. The horrendous working conditions in early industrial capitalism and the misery and unrest of a growing population could not be ignored any longer. A few philanthropic employers such as Charles Hindley in Britain and Daniel Legrand

---

Rights. The International Labour Organization and Beyond (Basingstoke: Palgrave Macmillan; Geneva: ILO); Jensen, J.; Lichtenstein,N. (eds.) (2015) *The ILO from Geneva to the Pacific Rim. West Meets East* (Basingstoke: Palgrave Macmillan; Geneva: ILO); Boris, E., Hoehtker, D. Zimmerann, S. (eds) (2018) *Women's ILO. Transnational Networks, Global Labour Standards and Gender Equality, 1919 to the Present*. Studies in Global Social History (Leiden: Brill; Geneva: ILO).

[5] Maul, D. (2019), *The International Labour Organization: 100 Years of Global Social Policy* (Berlin: De Gruyter/Geneva: ILO); Kott, S (2018) 'La justice sociale dans un monde global: l'Organisation internationale du Travail (19192019)', *Le mouvement social* (special issue), no. 263/2.

[6] Today, the employers in the ILO are represented by the International Organization of Employers (IOE), created in 1920, the workers by their most representative trade union confederations, affiliated to the International Trade Union Confederation (ITUC).

in France were the first to claim the reduction of working time and a ban on child labour, and this not only through national factory laws, but also through international agreements. Inspired by the anti-slavery movement, and against the backdrop of a first wave of globalisation, they understood that only international regulation could avoid the distortion of unfair competition and disadvantages for socially progressive nations.

In the following decades a broader social reform movement emerged in a number of industrialised, mostly European countries. Doctors, academics, jurists and enlightened industrialists pushed governments to adopt the first labour and social insurance laws. Humanitarian and Christian motives played a role, together with the objective of preserving and increasing workers' productivity and of preventing strikes and social unrest.

These social reform networks became more international in outlook and action. At the end of the 19th century, the first international associations were created, most importantly, in 1900, the International Association for Labour Legislation (IALL). It became a blueprint for the future ILO. The IALL convened international conferences where governments negotiated the first international agreements, the first one being a convention to prohibit white phosphorus, which was adopted in 1906.[7]

The most important actor in the struggle for better working conditions were the reform-oriented segments of a growing, albeit heterogeneous, labour movement and their trade union allies. They claimed not only better working conditions, but also fundamental rights such as freedom of association. While trade union action had mostly a local or national horizon, the first international umbrella organisations, accompanied by the growing interest in international regulations, were created after the turn of the century.

---

[7] Kott, S. (2014) 'From transnational reformist network to International Organization: the International Association for Labour Legislation and the International Labour Organization (1900-1930)', in B. Struck, D. Rodogno and J. Vogel (eds.) *Shaping the Transnational Sphere* (NYC: Berghahn Books), 239–258.

The decisive factors for the creation of the ILO were WWI and the Bolshevik revolution in Russia. Reformist trade unions gained considerable leverage in the belligerent countries, and representatives of the international trade union movement met in Leeds (1916) and Berne (1917) to claim a permanent structure devoted to the international regulation of labour issues. Their demands gained weight at the end of the war, when misery and dissatisfaction grew by the day.[8] The Bolshevik revolution of 1917 provided a catalyst for social uprisings in other countries and the fears this caused added weight to the voice of the reformist labour movements.

In the spring of 1919 widespread social unrest, exacerbated by the Spanish Flu, and millions of returning soldiers under weapons, created an explosive situation which pushed the Allied governments to create, through part XIII of the Treaty of Versailles, the ILO as an autonomous agency of the new League of Nations. The ILO's international tripartism was a revolutionary design, based on the unprecedented wartime experiences of cooperation between employers and workers in some of the belligerent countries. Class compromise was seen as a remedy against revolution. The new ILO was immediately denounced by the communists, who accused it of betraying the working class.

3. The interwar years: Expanding workers' protection in an unstable world

The ILO stood for the ambitious objective to create "humane conditions of labour"[9] in an open capitalist economy. For the first time, social justice was seen as an essential condition for lasting peace.

---

[8] Tosstorff, R. (2005) 'The International Trade-Union Movement and the Founding of the International Labour Organization', *International Review of Social History*, 50(3), 399-433.

[9] ILO, *Constitution of the International Labour Organisation* (Paris, 1919). The current constitution of 1946 can be found on the ILO website.

The main means to put this mandate into practice was the elaboration of universally applicable international labour standards (binding conventions and non-binding recommendations), most often initiated by the workers and usually contested by the employers.[10] They were based on extensive research and statistical work carried out by the International Labour Office. Since international labour standards are adopted and their application is monitored by the International Labour Conference (ILC), where delegations are composed of workers', employers' and government representatives according to a 2:1:1 ratio, they have until today a unique legitimation.

The early labour standards[11] fulfilled the most urgent demands of the labour movement, most importantly the Hours of Work Convention No. 1. They aimed, first, to improve working conditions and protect the most vulnerable workers, such as women and minors, and second, to establish basic economic security for workers through conventions on wage-fixing and social insurance.

Under its first director, Albert Thomas from France, the ILO embarked almost immediately on a course of constant expansion of its mandate. Its standards gradually covered more and more diverse groups of wage workers, not only industrial workers and the truly "international workers" – seafarers and migrants – , but also workers in agriculture, offices and commerce. The conventions on colonial labour, most prominently the Forced Labour Convention No. 29, of 1930, were a special case, since they tried to abolish inhumane exploitative practices, anticipating the human rights dimension of later conventions, and to transform indigenous labour into a special type of contractual wage work, which was less regulated.

---

[10] For the role of the workers in the ILO, see Tapiola, K. (2019) *The Driving Force. Birth and Evolution of Tripartism – The Role of the ILO's Workers' Group* (Geneva: ILO).

[11] All ILO instruments can be found at https://www.ilo.org/dyn/normlex/en/f?p=NORMLEXPUB:1:0::NO:::.

The economic crisis of the 1930s and the resulting mass-unemployment pushed the ILO to expand its mandate beyond the regulation of working conditions. Under the leadership of Albert Thomas' successor, Harold Butler from Britain, it committed itself to a programme inspired by Keynesianism. It included the promotion of public work schemes and the adoption of further conventions on social insurance and the limitation of working time, to stimulate demand.

Between 1919 and 1939, the ILO adopted an impressive 66 conventions. In 1926, in order to cope with the reporting obligations of member States that had ratified conventions, it created a supervisory system.[12] However, despite Albert Thomas' tireless campaigning, the ratification rate increased only slowly. Many countries feared to lose their competitive advantage as long as major industrial powers would not ratify. This was especially the case with Convention No. 1 on the Eight-hour-work day. Others stated that local conditions did not allow them to adapt national labour legislation to ILO standards.

From the beginning, the fact that not all member States had the same level of social and economic development represented a challenge to the universality of ILO standards. In order to address this problem, the ILO sent technical assistance missions, first to Greece, in 1930, and later especially to Latin American countries. ILO officials, who were often renowned experts in their field, helped with drafting labour codes and setting up social security systems, labour inspection, labour departments, etc.[13]

These activities were also proof of the ILO's move away from Europe, where authoritarian and fascist regimes oppressed and persecuted trade unions and refused international cooperation. Ties

---

[12] ILO (2019) *The rule of the game* (Geneva: ILO).

[13] Plata-Stenger, V. (2020) *Social Reform, Modernization and Technical Diplomacy* (Berlin, Boston: De Gruyter Oldenbourg).

with member States in Latin America and Asia became stronger and the ILO's affinity with the New Deal policies of the Roosevelt administration led to a long-lasting close cooperation with the United States. They finally joined the ILO in 1934, together with the Soviet Union, after Nazi Germany had left.

4. War and exile

With the outbreak of WWII in 1939, the League of Nations went into rapid decline. In 1940, the ILO had to leave Switzerland, then besieged by Germany and its Allies. John Winant from the US, third ILO director, negotiated the transfer of a reduced number of staff to Montreal, Canada. While International Labour Conferences were suspended, technical assistance continued. Under his successor, Edward Phelan from Ireland, and as early as 1941, during a special conference in New York City, the ILO, which had positioned itself firmly on the side of the Allied forces and was supported by the US government, started to claim its role in post-war reconstruction.

The most important event during the wartime exile was the ILC convened in Philadelphia in October 1944. The famous Declaration[14], was negotiated by the tripartite delegations of 41 out of 51 ILO member States. Drawing the lessons from the social and economic crisis which had led to fascism, war and genocide, it was a visionary document which broadened the ILO's mandate of social justice. All policies, "in particular those of an economic and financial character", should be scrutinised from now on in the light of an overriding social objective.

---

[14] "Declaration Concerning the Aims and Purposes of the International Labour Organisation", in ILO, 26th Session (1944), *Record of Proceedings*, App. XIII, 621-623.

The Declaration positioned the ILO at the forefront of the emerging human rights discourse, defining social justice in terms of individual human rights, which appeared for the first time in an international document and prepared the ground for the Universal Declaration of Human Rights four years later: "All human beings, irrespective of race, creed or sex, have the right to pursue both their material well-being and their spiritual development in conditions of freedom and dignity, of economic security and equal opportunity", states the Philadelphia Declaration. The ILO reconfirmed its commitment to the notion that "labour is not a commodity" and to policies of (partial) decommodification.

By stating that "poverty anywhere constitutes a danger to prosperity everywhere", the Declaration had a global vision. A fair post-war economic order should bring economic security for all workers through full employment (which legitimised the expansion of the ILO's much contested engagement with employment policies) and the "extension of social security measures to provide a basic income to all in need of such protection and comprehensive medical care" (which provided a blueprint of the modern welfare State, based on New Deal policies and European social reform concepts).

Finally, the Declaration reconfirmed the ILO's commitment to tripartite cooperation, which had not made much progress on the national level prior to the war. This meant strengthening the role of free trade unions and promoting the principle of freedom of association. After the experience of totalitarian regimes and in the emerging Cold War confrontation, employers were ready to support both.

Despite many setbacks and against the will of the Soviet Union, the ILO was accepted in 1946 as the first specialised agency of the United Nation and annexed the Declaration of Philadelphia to its Constitution. In 1947, the Office returned to Geneva.

5. Cold War, decolonisation and the neoliberal turn

The 40-year period between the end of WWII and the fall of the Berlin Wall was defined by three overlapping and interrelated developments which had a major impact on the ILO's activities. The first one was the Cold War. The ILO, although firmly rooted in the camp of Western free market democracies, became an arena of the Cold War confrontation, especially after the Soviet Union resumed its membership in 1954. But the Cold War also benefitted the ILO, especially the workers' group, because it increased the willingness of Western employers to cooperate. This was beneficial for the ILO's standard-setting activities, which accelerated and diversified. Shared beliefs in productivity, rationalisation and industrialisation as the best means to achieve social progress provided opportunities for dialogue and cooperation despite the political confrontation.

The second development was the decolonisation process, which accelerated following India's independence in 1947. In 1960 alone, 15 African States joined the ILO. It adapted with the creation of regional offices and the establishment of regular regional conferences. Decolonisation changed the power balance within the UN system and the ILO. Developing countries had now the majority and wanted to give priority to their economic development.

The third development was economic. WWII was followed in many countries by a long boom period, based on the need to reconstruct, on technological progress and cheap oil. Welfare capitalism, inspired by Keynesian principles, flourished in the Northern hemisphere, where full employment was almost achieved and industrial relations made solid progress. The standard of living increased also in Socialist countries, and some developing countries achieved considerable growth rates. In the mid-1970s, the oil crises ended the "thirty golden years". An economic recession started for which the remedy was no longer being sought in polices inspired by Keynesianism, but in neoliberal free market polices.

During the first post war decade, the ILO had to position itself in the emerging multilateral system of the United Nations, where the Soviet Union was using ECOSOC to limit the ILO's competences as much as possible. Under the leadership of US Director-General David Morse, who was elected in 1948, standard setting was put on a new human rights basis.

In the decade between 1948 and 1958, the ILO translated important principles of its Constitution and the Declaration of Philadelphia into labour standards. Conventions No. 87 on freedom of association and No. 98, on the right to organise and collective bargaining, adopted in 1948 and 1949, codified freedom of association as the most important of all labour rights, since it "enables" workers to realize further social and economic rights. To support this principle, the ILO created in 1951 a special body to deal with complaints, the tripartite Committee on Freedom of Association (CFA).

Freedom of association and the question of representation became one of the major points of conflict with the Soviet Union and other socialist countries, where trade unions were under centralised control and independent employers did not exist. However, the growth of the public sector with managers rather than private employers in many capitalist countries allowed the ILO in the end to apply a flexible definition of tripartism, which covered socialist economies as well. In the beginning of the 1980s, Conventions No. 87 and 98, which had been ratified by the socialist countries, became a major reference in the battle for the recognition of Poland's independent trade union "Solidarnosc". This was eventually an important step towards the end of the communist regimes in Poland and elsewhere in Europe.

The Abolition of Forced Labour Convention No. 107, adopted in 1957, benefited from the Cold War context. Against the backdrop of the still fresh experience of Nazi labour camps and the existence of Soviet gulags, forced labour was reframed as a human rights issue. Since the Convention banned forced labour not only as a political punishment, which put the Soviet Union on the defensive, but also as a means of development, it soon became a controversial topic for developing countries which considered certain forms of compulsory labour as necessary for their economic development.

In 1951 and 1958 the ILO adopted two conventions codifying the human right of non-discrimination and equal treatment. Convention No. 100 on equal remuneration was an important step forward in the fight for equal rights for women in the world of work, leading the ILO out of the phase of more protection-oriented standard setting in the interwar period. The Discrimination (Employment and Occupation) Convention (No. 111) broadened the fight against discrimination by including other forms, such as discrimination for reasons of religion, political opinion, national origin, colour and race. The latter allowed socialist countries, together with the workers, to successfully push through the Convention against the resistance of the US and the colonial powers, where racial discrimination was a reality. The Convention underpinned the ILO's fight against apartheid in South Africa, which gained momentum in the 1960s and eventually led to the country's withdrawal from the ILO. It returned with the end of apartheid in 1994.

Decolonisation transformed the ILO. Its membership increased rapidly, from 55 members in 1948 to 121 in 1970.[15] While the ILO became a more universal organisation, the universality of its standards was challenged. During its first decades, it had addressed the needs of (mostly male) workers in the industrialised countries and promoted a model of formal, contract-based employment, with rights and protections. However, the economy of developing countries was

---

[15] Ghebali (1989), 119-120.

characterised by large scale informality in the form of small enterprises and subsistence agriculture with generally low productivity. Formal employment was rare and un- and underemployment – if measurable at all – were widespread, as was poverty, despite the economic growth that took place.

This made it difficult to put into practice the labour standards which the new member States had ratified with optimism and confidence. Therefore, in the unfolding competition between a Western and a socialist path to development, the ILO made technical cooperation the second most important area of its activities. Its growing importance led to major changes also in the Office, where economists played an increasingly important role. In 1960, the ILO created an International Institute for Labour Studies. Devoted to research and training, it put a strong focus on development issues.

After the war, the European Recovery Programme (ERP) had given a boost to the technical assistance activities of the ILO. Under the leadership of David Morse, the ILO broadened this area of activity beyond the European context and linked it to US development policies, based on US president Truman's 1949 Five Point Speech. The orientation towards the less developed countries was an important step in positioning the ILO within the UN system, especially after its claim to become an international agency for migration had failed because of the Cold War tensions.

The ILO's technical assistance programme (TAP), which started in 1949, was based on modernisation theory and its assumption that all countries would repeat in accelerated form the development of industrialised countries. In the 1950s, the various TAP projects were mainly focussing on vocational training, health and safety at the workplace and industrial relations. Their objective was to build a modern industrial workforce in order to promote growth and productivity.

Financed by the UN's Expanded Programs of Technical Assistance, these projects were rather small. The Andean Indian Programme (1953-1962) was an exception, since it had an integrated approach. In collaboration with other UN agencies, it addressed economic, social and medical issue, in order to lead the "backward" native Indian populations in a number of Latin American countries towards integration in their respective national societies, with rather mixed results.

Thanks to the creation of the United Nations development programme (UNDP) in 1965, the ILO could massively expand its development projects in the 1960s and 1970s. They were further supported by the International Training Centre in Turin, which opened in 1965 and provided vocational training to educators from the developing world.

Already in the 1960s, however, the hope that industrial growth and the building of a modern industrial sector would quickly absorb the rural labour force proved wrong. The situation was further aggravated by continued population growth. Developing countries criticised their continued structural disadvantage in the "neo--colonial" division of labour. In 1964, they formed Group 77 at the UN, to voice their demand of a "right to development". A decade later, they proposed a New International Economic Order, which was adopted by the UN General Assembly in 1974, but countered by the group of the most advanced Industrial Market Economies (IMEC). These divisions contributed, in addition to the Cold War tensions, to conflict and politicisation in the ILO. Among other things, they led to the temporary withdrawal of the United States between 1977 and 1980.

In this context, the ILO shifted its development approach. With its 1964 Employment Policy Convention (No. 122), which was largely tailored to the needs of the developing world, it put emphasis on the creation of "full, productive and freely chosen employment".

When the ILO celebrated its 50th anniversary, it not only received the Nobel Peace Prize, but also launched an ambitious World Employment Programme (WEP). The aim was to find out why the growth models that had essentially been transferred from the industrial countries had failed to generate employment and alleviate poverty in the developing world.

This innovative programme, which was not without its critics in the ILO and especially in the United States, combined employment missions, research and policy advise. It stood for a new appreciation of the informal economy, which it conceptualised for the first time. It drew attention to the rural economy and the role of women in development. It promoted economic planning and redistribution and made the fulfilment of basic needs (food security, housing, education, public health, transport) an essential precondition for successful employment policies. The WEP also promoted "appropriate technology" as complementary to capital-intensive industrialisation. With the World Employment Conference, held in 1976, the WEP reached its high point. It continued to influence development research and employment polices well into the 1980s, but the tide had already started to change.[16]

Many developing countries were hit hard by the oil crisis and the resulting economic downturn. They were accumulating debts. Inflation and unemployment returned to the industrialised countries. What was less clearly seen at the time was the paradigm change under way. In order to counter the crisis and promote growth, all barriers to what we now call "globalisation" were removed little by little in the 1970s and 1980s, starting with the deregulation of the financial sector after the end of the Bretton Woods system. In

---

[16] Sollai, M. (2019) 'The World Employment Programme. Past, Present and Future' (Geneva: ILO) https://www.ilo.org/wcmsp5/groups/public/ed_emp/documents/genericdocument/wcms_706830.pdf

the late 1970s, many governments, most prominently the UK under
Margaret Thatcher and the US during Ronald Reagan's presidency,
but also such international financial institutions as the IMF and the
World Bank, turned to neoliberal free market policies which embraced privatisation, deregulation, a "streamlining" of the welfare
State and the liberalisation of trade and capital flows. When the
first debt crisis broke out in Mexico in 1982, the IMF and the World
Bank imposed Structural Adjustment Programmes in exchange for
loans. Structural adjustment became a standard recipe for crisis-
-ridden countries in the following decades.

The ILO reacted slowly to this paradigm change, which it could
not directly influence and which stood in clear opposition to many
of its central values, most importantly the regulation of labour markets, collective bargaining and democratic decision making, and the
central role of the State in economic planning and social protection.

Under French Director-General Francis Blanchard, technical
cooperation and standard setting expanded, with attention paid to
emerging new problems: on one hand, the multinational enterprises, which started to challenge the national framework of the ILO's
standard setting[17], and, on the other hand, working conditions,
which had deteriorated due to continued technological change,
rationalisation and automation.

Most importantly, during the 1970s and 1980s the ILO engaged
in democratic transition processes in a number of countries. It was
part of an international coalition against apartheid in South Africa
and supported trade unions in Poland, Portugal, Spain and Greece
in their fight against non-democratic regimes. In Latin America,
especially in Chile and Argentina, where dictatorial regimes came

---

[17] In 1977, the ILO's Governing Body adopted a "Tripartite Declaration of
Principles, concerning Multinational Enterprises and Social Policy", consisting of a
set of international guidelines, linked to ILO standards.

to power, it supported trade unions in their struggle for freedom of association. The human rights principles and conventions of the immediate post-war decades were put to the test.

6. Globalisation and reorientation

With the end of the Cold War, the ILO under its new Director-General Michel Hansenne from Belgium, had to react to the uncertainties of the emerging new international political order. After the disintegration of the Soviet Union and, a few years later, of Yugoslavia, 26 new member States joined the ILO. A new regional office in Budapest was set up in 1993 to promote tripartite cooperation, but the ILO could do little to ease the transition from socialist to open market economies, which primarily consisted of a neoliberal shock therapy of structural adjustment, causing unemployment and poverty.

With the end of the Cold War, the last barriers to globalisation fell. This increased the power of the IMF and the World Bank, which were joined in 1995 by the WTO as the third pillar of an international economy reorganised under neoliberal auspices. The idea of international regulation of work was seen as an obstacle to globalisation and global competition – its all-encompassing principle. The disconnect between the economic and political sphere, with the latter in the role of supporting the former, and deep hostility against the labour movement were at the core of the neoliberal belief system. It was in almost every way the opposite of the ideas formulated in Philadelphia.[18]

With the disappearance of its communist counter model of social-economic organisation, for many the ILO had lost its *raison*

---

[18] Slobodian, Q. (2018), *The Globalists. The End of Empire and the Roots of Neoliberalism* (Cambridge M.A.: Harvard University Press).

d'être. Employers and many governments, from industrialised but also developing countries, now openly criticised the ILO's standard setting, especially the binding conventions: too many, too technical, and often outdated. They also pointed to declining ratification rates, which allegedly proved that there was a decreasing interest in binding standards. Therefore, they pushed for a substantial review of all labour standards, the promotion of a limited number of core labour standards, based on larger human rights principles, and priority for non-binding instruments and corporate social responsibility (CSR).[19]

In his report to the ILC in 1994, the year of the ILO's 75th anniversary, Hansenne proposed not only a large scale review of the standard system[20], but also the refocusing on four fundamental, human rights-based principles: freedom of association, the elimination of child and forced labour and of all forms of discrimination at work. The related conventions should be promoted as a priority.[21] This re-orientation of the ILO's standards policy found its expression in the *Declaration on Fundamental Principles and Rights at Work*, adopted after heated debates by the ILC in 1998. It committed the member States to respecting the four fundamental principles, without directly imposing the ratification of the related conventions.

Two important developments led to the Declaration. First, the 1996 rejection, in Singapore, of a social clause in trade agreements

---

[19] H. G. Myrdal (1994) 'The ILO in the cross-fire: Would it survive the social clause?, in W. Sengenberger and D. Campbell (eds.), *International Labour Standards and Economic Interdependence* (Geneva: ILO), 339-356.

[20] Since 2017, the ILC can abrogate conventions which are in force. ILO (2019), 24.

[21] Today, the following conventions are considered as "fundamental": Freedom of Association and Protection of the Right to Organise Convention, 1948 (No. 87); Right to Organise and Collective Bargaining Convention, 1949 (No. 98); Forced Labour Convention, 1930 (No. 29) (and its 2014 Protocol); Abolition of Forced Labour Convention, 1957 (No. 105); Minimum Age Convention, 1973 (No. 138); Worst Forms of Child Labour Convention, 1999 (No. 182); Equal Remuneration Convention, 1951 (No. 100); Discrimination (Employment and Occupation) Convention, 1958 (No. 111).

by the First Ministerial Conference of the WTO, which considered the protection of core labour standards as an ILO area of competence. Developing countries feared that a social clause would be an instrument of protectionism and compromise their comparative advantage in the international competition. Second, the rejection, by the employers in the ILO, of any binding instrument. They favoured voluntary CSR initiatives and codes of conduct to address labour issues, especially in the expanding global supply chains.

The Declaration's follow-up heralded a new phase in the ILO's technical cooperation. Half of its budget was redirected to support the promotion of fundamental rights, most prominently the elimination of child and forced labour, which had reappeared as the dark side of globalisation. The Declaration repositioned the ILO in the new context of globalisation and enhanced its visibility. The ratification rates for the fundamental conventions went up. But it also had its critics. Some regretted the non-binding "soft law" character of the Declaration, seen as a concession to neoliberal forces and the United States. Others argued that it introduced a hierarchy of rights, which would mean a devaluation of traditional areas of the ILO's work, such as working conditions and social protection.[22] Yet another point of criticism was that the campaigns against child labour and forced labour mobilised huge resources whereas freedom of association was in comparison less promoted, although it was essential for the ILO and its vision of democratic decision making.

When Director-General Juan Somavia from Chile took office in 1999, it became clear that the previous year's Declaration could not be the only response to the social costs and the deep transformations caused by globalisation. While in some countries the standard

---

[22] In contrast to the fundamental Conventions, the vast majority of international labour standards adopted after WWII, including the ones on social security (such as Convention No. 102 of 1952) did not contain references to human rights, with the exception of the Employment Policy Convention (No.122) of 1964.

of living had increased, in many others inequalities deepened. The financialisation of the economy became an increasingly important feature of globalised capitalism. Its crises, such as the 1997 financial crisis in Asia, added to the social costs of globalisation. Precarious, informal work became more widespread[23] and trade union rights needed to be defended against ever more powerful global supply chains, where individual employers became invisible. Union membership decreased, especially in industrialised countries. As a result, workers and employers in the ILO were less and less representative of their respective constituencies. Last but not least, the environmental destruction caused by globalised capitalism could no longer be ignored.

To address the obvious unfairness of globalisation in a context of rising anti-globalisation militancy, Somavia introduced the Decent Work agenda in 1999. It redefined social justice in the 21st century and set four strategic objectives for all ILO members to pursue: employment, social protection, social dialogue, and rights at work.

The decent work approach aimed to reconcile two objectives which globalisation had put in conflict with each other: the protection of workers and the right to development. It had a clear focus on both sustainable development and the reduction of inequalities. For this very reason, the Declaration went beyond formal employment to include the workers in the informal economy.

The decent work concept was codified in the *Declaration on Social Justice for a Fair Globalization*, adopted in June 2008, a few months before one of the worst financial crises since 1945 broke out. In this context, the renewed focus on employment brought the ILO back to the international arena. Since 2009, it is invited to the G20 meetings.

---

[23] In 2018, the informal economy comprised around 60% of the global workforce. ILO (2018) *Women and men in the informal economy: a statistical picture* (third edition) (Geneva: ILO).

Both declarations constitute the framework in which ILO's activities have evolved in the two decades leading up to its Centenary. Standard setting has slowed down significantly, with a tendency towards broader conventions and non-binding recommendations. Since 2008, the ILO has adopted only three conventions: In 2011 a Domestic Worker Convention, No. 189, which presented a first step towards the regulation of the informal economy; in 2014 a Protocol to Forced Labour Convention No. 29 of 1930, which now includes human trafficking; and finally, in 2019, Convention No. 190 on violence and harassment.

Technical cooperation activities linked to the four strategic objectives have evolved and diversified, currently totalling 693 projects world-wide[24]. Under the ILO's current Director-General Guy Ryder, who took office in 2012, decent work became goal no. 8 and an integral part of the UN's Sustainable Development Agenda 2030, adopted in 2015.

Within this framework, the ILO will need to prove the credibility of its mandate at a time when the continued rapid transformation of the world of work produces new forms of precarious work everywhere, when climate change and environmental destruction destroy livelihoods, when political conflict and war force millions to flee, and when COVID-19 brutally exacerbates existing inequalities, generating mass unemployment comparable to that of the 1930s.

At the beginning of a new century, the ILO has a historical chance to be part of a new paradigm that insists on the deep interlinkages between the economic, the social and the environmental dimensions of work. Traditional concepts of growth and progress have to be questioned in the light of these interdependencies.

---

[24] See the ILO Development Cooperation Dashboard https://www.ilo.org/Deve lopmentCooperationDashboard/#bsmphgd

7. Conclusion

When the ILO was founded in 1919, it was not at all obvious that it would have an impact or even survive. A new world order was emerging after a first global conflict of an unprecedented scale, in the middle of a flu pandemic which had cost a further 50 million lives. In 2020, in the midst of a new and very similar global virus, the ILO and the whole multilateral system is under enormous pressure. Since the end of the League of Nations, the ILO has resisted major shocks and changes and been at the forefront of social progress at various moments in time. It will need to demonstrate that it has this potential as it enters a new century.

COMMENT:

PORTUGAL IN THE CONTEXT OF ILO'S HISTORY

Álvaro Garrido[25] and António Rafael Amaro[26]

Dorothea Hoehtker's essay, "100 years of ILO – negotiating work in a changing world", offers an overview of the history of ILO while projecting its role, as a UN specialised agency, with regard to the future of work and social policies.

As recently as 2019 the ILO celebrated its first centenary. The occasion was an opportunity to evoke the institutional history of the main cycles of an international organisation that has been extremely important in terms of ensuring the dignity of work and the progress of social policies at the transnational level. Dorothea Hoehtker's essay clearly shows that the ILO's activity has always been deeply embedded in the major social and economic issues of each successive period and that the Organisation's primary mission – building social justice and ensuring the universal regulation of working conditions – remains indispensable and more pertinent than ever in these times of globalisation and pandemic.

The history of the ILO is so intertwined with the major crises of capitalism, the Second World War, the Cold War face-off, the

---

[25] University of Coimbra, Faculty of Economics, Center for Interdisciplinary Studies of the 20th Century.

[26] University of Coimbra, Faculty of Economics, Center for Interdisciplinary Studies of the 20th Century.

https://doi.org/10.14195/978-989-26-2277-4_2

decolonisation movements and, more recently, the resurgence of neoliberal ideas and globalisation, that to a large extent it overlaps with the very history of the 20th century. Hoehtker's piece stresses the fact that the ILO's inception took place under especially dramatic circumstances, marked by the imperfections of the peace-building process. The idea for an international bureau for labour-related issues stemmed, first and foremost, from an urgent double need: to build peace on the rubble of war and to check the spectre of revolution, Communism and anarcho-syndicalism, which threatened the liberal order and its institutions as they emerged from a long process of erosion and were faced with the perils of proletarian revolution. The idea for ILO was also born from a marked, reform-driven internationalist idealism that saw the universal regulation of working conditions and the construction of social policies based on positive law and humanist ethics as the foundations for the social progress that was required to achieve peace.

However, although the Great War, with its harrowing parade of social consequences – which struck at the same time as the "Spanish flu" and the Bolshevik Revolution of October 1917 – were decisive in establishing the ILO, the reasons for its creation also resided in the perception, by the liberal democracies that had emerged victorious from the war, that European and universal peace depended on how to solve the "social question", which in turn involved providing workers with reformist social laws, human dignity, and stronger ties to the State. Despite the internationalist rhetoric of Marxist worker organisations and the philanthropic and solidarity-driven solutions that promised workers paternalistic and mutualist solutions (Garrido, 2016: 77-96), the kind of impoverishment that was inherent in nineteenth-century industrial capitalism and the demand for better wages and improved working conditions brought the "social question" into the twentieth century. The need to address "the social question" forced the liberal State to come up with national and transnational reformist initiatives, notably in the domain of Social Law, a field that made unprecedented progress in France and other countries in the early twentieth century (Donzelot, 1994: 125-140).

Based on a tripartite model of representation that brought together workers, employers and States (Rodgers et alia, 2009: 12-15), the ILO was an expression of liberal parliamentary culture and called for transnational forms of consultation in the world of work. These new forms were to be built on consensus between the parties involved and to rest on "rational authority", two principles that are viewed by some authors as neo-corporatist. Furthermore, at its inception the ILO boldly appealed to a reformist multilateralism that was based on Social Law and made up of conventions and recommendations that sought to promote the creation of a kind of social and labour reformism increasingly woven into the different national legal corpora. Notwithstanding the difficulties and hesitations described in Dorothea Hoehtker's essay, this process was largely successful. Suffice it to mention the increase in inter-State regulatory norms and the steady building of a sort of international "Social Constitution" comprised of social and labour provisions in the codification of which the ILO has always played a major role (Rodrigues, 2013: 19).

The ILO's original Constitution (Part XIII of the Treaty of Versailles) brought together contributions from a variety of ideological sources. It defined itself, before anything else, by what it wished to fight and reject – mindless liberal individualism and, to an even greater extent, Bolshevik revolutionism and Anarchist chaos –, but its main underlying ideas were also very clear: Christian democracy, solidarity, and social liberalism (Rodgers et alia, 2009: 2). One could say that the ILO was an early expression of the internationalist social democracy that strove to save liberal democracies and capitalism itself from the crises that kept eroding them and from the threat of revolution (Hobsbawm, 1996).

The speech that accompanied the creation of the ILO and the entire Versailles peace process – a speech born of US President Woodrow Wilson's famous 14 points – made clear, in no uncertain terms, that a crucial short-term goal of the labour bureau should be to re-establish international trade, which in turn required a favourable social framework if it was to thrive (Rodgers et alia, 2009: 6). It was therefore no coincidence that hardly had the ILO been created when the Communist parties denounced it as a "bourgeois organisation" and a "betrayal of the working classes".

Portugal was among the founders of the ILO, which was established in 1919 under the League of Nations. An ally of the democratic powers that emerged victorious from World War I, the then young Portuguese Republic, although left drained by its exploits in the trenches and by the huge crisis caused by the war, was represented at the Paris Peace Conference.

Given its obligations as a member State and one of the founders of the ILO – one of the first intergovernmental agencies of the new "world order" that emerged from the First World War – Portugal was especially influenced by the ILO's recommendations and guidelines on national social policies. This impact can also be explained by the ILO's having taken a normative stance from very early on and by the fact that 1919 also happeend to be the year in which Portugal initiated a wide reformist programme in the social and labour sphere, through its recently created Ministry of Labour.

After the Republic was overthrown by a military coup that paved the way for a front of right-wing political sectors and interests headed by Salazar, everything the Republic had accomplished in terms of social policies, notably the legacy of the *Instituto Social de Seguros Obrigatórios* ("Social Institute of Compulsory Insurances"), soon came under attack. The latter's discontinuance meant the collapse of the first attempt at building a liberal welfare state and a huge setback for labour legislation. Once consolidated and enshrined in the Constitution, the Catholic and integralist dictatorship of the so called Estado Novo (Salazar's "New State") hastened to express its distrust of the country's commitments *vis-à-vis* the ILO.

The "corporatist law-based social State", established by the dictatorship in 1933, owed more to Italian fascism – with its rhetoric of a "nationalisation of labour" – and to the counter-revolutionary papal encyclicals than to the principles of labour law that the ILO's normativity had contributed to internationalise and thanks to which the "social and democratic rule of law" as defined by Habermas was to come into being.

Cristina Rodrigues's doctoral thesis, entitled *Portugal and the ILO (1933-1974)*, thoroughly analysed this paradoxical tension between, on the one hand, the hostility of the *Estado Novo* towards the ILO's cosmopolitan and liberal-democratic normativity and, on the other, the growing juridification of the Portuguese dictatorship's labour field. In fact, despite its corporatist ideology, which entailed a unique and constrained version of labour relations, the dictatorship took a cynical approach to international labour law by reacting unevenly to the conventions issued by the ILO. As might be expected, only a small number of conventions on "human rights and rights at work" were ratified, as they involved normative discussions on the issue of "forced labour" in the African colonies, work-related discrimination against "indigenous and tribal peoples", freedom of association, the right to collective bargaining, and child labour. In the period between 1933 and 1974, Portugal only ratified eight out of 29 conventions pertaining to these issues (Rodrigues, 2013: 135-136).

As pointed out in Rodrigues's dissertation, in the aftermath of the Second World War and the difficult times with which the ILO was faced after 1939, it entered a new cycle, inspired by the 1944 Declaration of Philadelphia and the adherence to principles and demands of social justice later to be enshrined in the Universal Declaration of Human Rights.

This new humanist impetus on the part of the ILO, combined with the establishment of democratic Welfare States in various European countries and the wave of decolonisation that marked the Cold War years, caused Portugal – a dictatorial and corporatist regime that had outlived Europe's fascisms – to find itself in an even more difficult situation with respect to its relationship with the ILO. The concept of "universal social rights" enshrined in the ILO's 1946 Constitution, as well as the demand for — or, at least, the expectation of having — Keynesian social policies at the centre of the economies of its member States, were the polar opposite of the realities obtaining in Portugal, which continued to view international labour conventions as a form of interference in domestic issues (Rodrigues, 2013: 140-141).

When the ILO entered this new phase of normative dynamics, based on the socio-labour manifestation of work-related human rights and the realities of the emerging post-colonial world, Portugal was faced with considerable international pressure having to do with the issue of "forced labour" in the colonies, as a result of which the country found itself increasingly isolated.

By putting an end to 48 years of dictatorship, the revolution of 25 April, 1974 opened the way to a new relationship, one of greater cooperation and trust, between Portugal and the ILO, not least because the new democratic system placed freedom of association and workers' rights among its priorities. The demand for full freedom for trade unions was made two days into the "Carnation Revolution", as part of a manifesto presented at a meeting that also marked the public emergence of Intersindical as a major trade union federation (Brito and Rodrigues, 2013). The right to establish free trade unions and the right to strike – two crucial principles enshrined in several ILO conventions that pre-1974 Portugal had refused to sign – were finally ratified during the first years of the revolution. Such was the case with Convention No. 135 on Workers' Representatives, which was ratified in 1976, and Convention No. 87 (ILO, 1948), on Feedom of Association and Protection of the Right to Organise, ratified in 1977.

The establishment of democracy and the social rights enshrined in the country's 1976 Democratic Constitution were in line with the ILO's most progressive positions and recommendations, notably with regard to labour rights and social protection. Furthermore, they helped ensure that Portugal, albeit belatedly and not in sync with Europe's most advanced countries, created the institutional pillars of the Social Rule of Law, as had been the case with demoliberal countries following World War II (Amaro, 2018). This happened in the areas of health, education and social security.

The political and institutional situation generated by the newly established democratic system, combined with the new Constitution (1976) and the joining of the then European Economic Community (1986), completely changed the country's relationship with the ILO. The results became immediately visible in such important aspects as the ease with which conventions were now ratified – a sign that the distrust that had characterised the long period in which Salazar (1933-1968) and Marcelo Caetano (1968-1974) had been at the head of the *Estado Novo* had finally come to an end. Recent studies (Rodrigues, 2019; Ferreira, 2019) have shown that the new period was characterised by enhanced institutional and political collaboration, as illustrated by the rise in the number of ratifications and by the fact that the time lapse between approval of new conventions by the ILO and their incorporation into the national legal system became increasingly shorter. Twenty nine conventions were ratified in the 1980s alone. Eight more were ratified in the following decade and 14 since the start of the new millennium. These figures show that Portugal stands now among the countries

with the highest number of ILO directives inscribed in their socio-
-labour legal framework.

Life has not been easy for the socio-labour world these past few decades. As a result of the financialisation of the economy, of globalised capitalism with its inherent social costs – particularly the crisis of social protection systems –, of job insecurity, and of the difficulties experienced by the trade union movement and the downturn in union representation, the ILO is faced with serious challenges. But it is precisely at difficult moments like this that the ILO tends to assert and consolidate itself, as has been often the case in the past. In a context like the present one, in which decent and sustainable work for all remains a difficult and elusive goal, the pressure and the expectations with which organisations like the ILO have to deal tend to increase. As has also been the case throughout its century-long history, the ILO is expected to provide us with responses at once firm, politically consistent, and capable of overcoming socio-labour deregulation, the decrease in union membership and trade union power, job insecurity, and increasing inequality. It is our belief that the ILO's credibility in the future will depend on its ability to show that it is up to this challenge. As it turns 100, the ILO is faced with a historic opportunity to accomplish something which, given its history as an important international organisation, can only prove feasible: to embrace a new consensus aimed at combating work without rights, economic growth without social and environmental responsibility, and the new social and labour inequalities, thereby contributing to a fairer world.

References:

Amaro, António Rafael (2018), "The Late Construction of Portugal Welfare State: The Failure of the Social Corporatist State (1933-1974)", *Memoria y Civilización*, 21, 437-454.

Brito, José Maria Brandão; Rodrigues, Cristina (2013), *A UGT na história do movimento sindical português, 1970-1990*. Lisboa: Tinta-da-China.

Castel, Robert (1995), *Les Métamorphoses de la Question Sociale*. Paris: Fyard

Ferreira, António Casimiro (org.) (2019), *A Organização Internacional do Trabalho Português – Reflexos e Limitações de um Paradigma Sociojurídico*. Coimbra, Almedina e Centro de Estudos Sociais.

Garrido, Álvaro (2016), *Cooperação e Solidariedade — Uma História da Economia Social*. Lisboa: Tinta da China.

Hobsbawm, Eric (1996), *The Age of Extremes — A History of the World, 1914-1991*. London: Vintage.

Rodgers, Gerry; Lee, Eddy; Swepston, Lee; Van Daele, Jasmien (2009), *The ILO and the Quest for Social Justice, 1919-2009*. Geneva: International Labour Office.

Rodrigues, Cristina (2013), *Portugal e a Organização Internacional do Trabalho (1933-1974)*. Porto: Edições Afrontamento.

Rodrigues, Cristina (2019), «Largos dias têm cem anos – Portugal e a OIT», *in* Ferreira, António Casimiro (org.), *A Organização Internacional do Trabalho Português – Reflexos e Limitações de um Paradigma Sociojurídico*. Coimbra: Almedina e Centro de Estudos Sociais, 17-33.

CHAPTER 2

THE ILO, DECENT WORK AND MULTILATERALISM[27]

Kirsten-Maria Schapira-Felderhoff[28]

1. Introduction: Context

Inequality is a defining challenge of our time. Recent waves of globalization, notably in international trade and finance, have done much to reduce global inequality, and yet within countries, the gap between richest and poorest is widening. While extreme poverty has been reduced, income and wealth are increasingly concentrated. Most economies are growing, but the labour share of national income is declining, and large portions of the world's workforce have experienced real wage stagnation. And while women's economic contributions are growing, gender inequalities are persistent. All this has led to the growth of damaging and unacceptable inequalities, a situation where everybody loses (108th Session of the International Labour Conference; remarks in the context of the panel on "Multilateralism towards equal work").

---

[27] This paper was received in June 2020 (originally in Spanish language) and corresponds to the participation in the seminar "Decent Work and Multilateralism" (2nd edition of "Cátedra OIT/ILO Chair"), held at the University of Coimbra, Faculty of Economics (FEUC), on 21 February 2019.

[28] Senior Specialist for Standards and Human Rights, Relations with Intergovernmental Organizations, Multilateral Cooperation Department, International Labour Organization.

https://doi.org/10.14195/978-989-26-2277-4_3

Some African countries have some of the world's fastest-growing and most unequal economies. They have come to the realisation that development is not the same as strong economic growth, because strong economic growth does not automatically lead to shared growth. The best definition of inclusive growth, and also the simplest, is the creation of decent jobs.

2. The ILO and decent work: the conceptual framework

The International Labour Organization (ILO), a specialised UN agency, was established in 1919. Thanks to its unique tripartite nature, governments, employers and workers are brought together and represented in its executive bodies.

According to its Constitution, it is the mission of the International Labour Organization to promote social justice. At a time when the workers of industrialised nations were being exploited, ILO's founders understood the importance of social justice as a precondition for peace. Security, humanitarian, political and economic considerations led to the creation of ILO. Another reason was the growing awareness of worldwide economic interdependence and of the need for cooperation if similar working conditions were to obtain in the countries that compete for markets.

The ILO advocates the concept of decent work as a way of opening up a social dimension to the globalisation process and as a framework for its initiatives in support of national policy goals. The term "Decent Work" was coined in a June 1999 Report submitted by the Director-General to the ILO's 87th session.

The origins of the concept date back to the Declaration of Philadelphia, which gave the Organization a mandate that laid the foundations of decent work, sixty years before the concept received its current name. The notion conveys the broad and multiple aspects associated with today's work, encapsulated in a phrase to which everyone can relate and which seeks to express, in broad terms, what a good job or dignified work should be like in this globalised world of ours.

The underlying assumption is that both men and women be given the opportunity to perform a productive activity for which they get fair wages, job security and social protection. Furthermore, they are to be provided with increased prospects for personal development and social integration and the right to participation and association, as well as the guarantee of equal treatment for all.

Always respecting the need for gender equality, four strategic objectives are implicit in the decent work agenda: rights at work, employment opportunities, social protection, and social dialogue. Each objective plays a specific role in achieving broader goals, such as social inclusion, the eradication of poverty, the strengthening of democracy, full personal development, and personal fulfilment.

In short, decent work has contributed to the building of bridges between the ILO's historical concerns and the contemporary challenges resulting from the need for social justice. In so doing, it contributes to the international attainment of another objective: to establish a direct link between the economic development of societies and the labour rights of the individuals who make them up.

3. Making decent work a global goal

From its outset, the concept of decent work has gained international currency in order to define the set of characteristics that any employment relationship that meets international labour standards is supposed to cover. Furthermore, such acceptance has been repeatedly recognised at all levels.

As a consequence, decent work considerations have become a larger part of the policies and activities of UN agencies, funds and programmes. They have led to new development objectives and initiatives and have figured prominently in the international development debate, especially during the economic and financial crisis. Thus, decent work has been reaffirmed as an objective, for example, in a number of resolutions of the UN General Assembly, and by the European Economic and Social Committee and in the context of world summits and major regional and international bodies. Furthermore, during the financial crisis these objectives were frequently invoked as part of policy responses.

4. Decent work *vis-à-vis* the 2030 Agenda for Sustainable Development and its 17 Goals

Decent work provides individuals, families and communities with the necessary means to meet their social and economic needs and aspirations, improve their lives, and generate new options and opportunities.

Given that jobs connect people to society, to the economy and to the environment, decent work has implications for the economic, social and environmental dimensions of sustainable development. Therefore, decent work is a key global demand in our changing world; it is based on fundamental values and principles and its objective is indivisible and universal in scope.

This is why ILO's concept of decent work is inscribed in the United Nations development framework as enshrined in the 2030 Agenda for Sustainable Development and its 17 Goals (SDGs).

In other words, the 2030 Agenda for Sustainable Development is a policy document that every country should use to shape its own national sustainable development strategies, so that they will ultimately fit into a universal, global strategy that is greater than the sum of its parts. It puts people and the planet centre stage and provides the international community with the impetus it needs to work in unison towards addressing the enormous challenges facing humanity, including those pertaining to the world of work. Besides, it recognises that social development and social justice are of critical importance for the achieving and maintaining of peace and security both at the domestic and international level and, conversely, that social development and social justice cannot be achieved if there is no peace, security, or respect for all human rights and fundamental freedoms.

The importance of decent work for sustainable development is particularly evident in Goal 8. Aimed at "promoting inclusive and sustainable economic growth, employment and decent work for all", this goal is a key commitment of the ILO and its constituents. Other key elements of decent work are also widely woven into many of the other 16 goals of the UN's current vision of development.

In sum, decent work has been turned into a global objective and explicitly enshrined in the 2030 Agenda and its Sustainable Development Goals, as adopted by world leaders in September 2015.

5. The role of multilateralism in achieving the proposed goals based on the concept of decent work and the 2030 Agenda for Sustainable Development

As pointed out above, people around the world are faced with decent work deficits, inadequacies and exclusions. These may take the form of unemployment and underemployment, poor-quality and unproductive jobs, dangerous work and uncertain income, rights denied, gender inequality, the exploitation of migrant workers, lack of representation and voice, and inadequate protection and solidarity in case of disease, disability and old age.

Making decent work for all a global goal of the UN development framework as inscribed in the 2030 Agenda for Sustainable Development and its 17 Goals (SDGs) and making job creation a priority of economic policies and development plans will make it possible to create opportunities for decent work and also to create growth that is more robust, inclusive, and conducive to the reduction of inequalities. It is a virtuous circle that will ultimately benefit both the economy and people in general, while acting as an engine of sustainable growth.

Turning all this into a reality, however, calls for global attention and responsibility as well as global solutions and globally coordinated responses.

We know that no single institution can fight on its own. In order to address problems in their entirety, today's institutions need to act in conjunction.

This means that the multilateral system as a whole needs to take a concerted approach that allows the ILO to play a leading role in making sure that the Decent Work Agenda is in line with the strategies aimed at reducing poverty and achieving fair and inclusive globalisation.

By way of clarification: In the context and from the point of view of the United Nations, multilateralism is a system under which States are brought together to share a number of rules and commit to a set of equal and mutual obligations with the purpose of seeking and proposing coordinated responses at the global level.

Multilateralism thus stands in opposition to the notion that the rise in inequality "is the price we have to pay to keep the global economy growing." It entails the global "rules-based order" and its ultimate manifestation is the *United Nations System*, considered to be one of the greatest achievements of the 20th century.

It is true that in the current context, with the move towards a return to protectionism and the emergence of extremist political movements, there are sectors that question the effectiveness of multilateralism and its adequacy in an increasingly multipolar world.

However, despite all its limitations, international bodies have been and remain the site of dialogue among nations, cultures and religions, a forum where notable agreements have been struck and consolidated for the benefit of humanity.

Social dialogue is one of the basic elements of the concept of decent work, in that it offers concrete advantages for achieving sustainable development. These advantages have to do with, among other aspects, the inclusive nature of the social dialogue process and the way in which interactions get to be organised in that process.

In this connection the UN Secretary General, António Guterres, has stated: "Multilateralism remains the key factor in addressing our global challenges, making progress in terms of peacekeeping and security, protecting human rights and fostering sustainable development. With that in mind, the multilateral system, with the United Nations at its centre, supports countries in their effort to achieve sustainable development."

By the same token, the G20 forum has stressed the fact that "Effective multilateralism is more important than ever: Global challenges need global attention, global responsibility and global solutions. (...) With ongoing globalization and the impact of new technological changes, it remains our goal to promote decent work and quality jobs worldwide. Thus, we fully support the UN 2030 Agenda for Sustainable Development and the herein incorporated decent work agenda of the ILO."

Finally, with regard to the future of work and the challenges posed by it, the 2019 report of the ILO Global Commission on the Future of Work has stressed the importance of developing strategies within the multilateral framework on the future of work, by promoting social dialogue between governments and employers' and workers' organisations.

COMMENT:

DECENT WORK AND THE ILO'S TRANSCONSTITUTIONALISM OF SOCIAL INCLUSION

Marina Henriques[29] and António Casimiro Ferreira[30]

The decent work deficit, addressed in Kirsten-Maria Schapira-Felderhoff's 'The ILO, decent work and multilateralism', foregrounds the fact that workers are the most vulnerable group as far as the violation of fundamental rights is concerned. Contextual dynamics and the continuous crises they generate, which impact at both the global and national level, have repercussions in the area of labour rights. The recent pandemic has had uneven manifestations in different parts of the world, and its implications have been vastly different.

The data is out there and it shows that the problems in the domain of labour have worsened, as the decent work deficit continues to grow in a global context in which workers' rights are not enforced. In 2019, unemployment affected as many as 188 million workers across the world, which corresponds to a global unemployment rate of 5.4%. Many workers lacked decent working conditions – first and foremost, the more than 630 million (about 19% of the world's workers) who earn less than US$3.2 a day (ILO, 2020a: 12-13).

---

[29] University of Coimbra, Centre for Social Studies.

[30] University of Coimbra, Faculty of Economics, Centre for Social Studies.

https://doi.org/10.14195/978-989-26-2277-4_4

This situation has been made worse by the impacts of the COVID-19 pandemic, with 114 million jobs being lost from 2019 to 2020. In relative terms, job losses were higher for women (5.0 %) than for men and also higher for young workers (8.7%) than for older ones. In 2020, the global unemployment rate rose to 6.5% – a 1.1% increase (ILO, 2021). According to ILO estimates, the pandemic is still expected to consign 35 more million people to working poverty (ILO, 2020b: 3). The growing disconnect between the general principles of labour rights and real conditions on the ground has given rise to a proliferation of paradoxes involving various sources of normativity, such as, at the international level, the ILO and, at the national level, the legislative framework regulating labour relations in the member countries. Faced with these realities, the ILO's 109th International Labour Conference, held in 2021, adopted a Global Call to Action aimed at bringing about an inclusive, sustainable and resilient recovery from the pandemic crisis.

Lack of protection in the case of dismissal and the lack of access to social protection mechanisms by many workers when faced with unemployment lead to increased inequalities between different categories of workers and an increased risk of impoverishment and social exclusion. This gives rise to a complex social, legal and labour situation that has implications for the way in which society as a whole is organised and the way in which labour interactions take place in the context of democratic systems when viewed within the framework of national-international analytical tension.

In this context, the flexibilisation of rights, the deterioration of working and living conditions, the naturalisation of job insecurity and the rise in inequalities and unemployment should lead governments, social partners and international organisations to base their efforts on the defence of decent work. While public policies and the rights associated with them are structuring elements of the world of work, it is also true that they rest on the same tension that counterposes the national and the international sphere. This assumption opens up a path of reflection on the principle of respect for human dignity as it lies exposed to today's sinister and disruptive trend towards deregulation, flexibility and the challenges that face labour rights and that are expressed more and more frequently in legal formulas covering flexible, part-time and precarious work.

These reflections on the centrality of work and of work rights gives centre stage to the ILO's concept of the transconstitutionalism of social inclusion via the promotion of fundamental rights at work. The concept may be broadly defined – in contradistinction to the neoliberal model of global regulation – as the interweaving of ILO normativity and each specific national reality, with a view to the solving of problems pertaining to fundamental rights at work (Henriques, 2021).

The interaction between transnational and national dynamics of the creation, enforcement and mobilisation of labour rights foregrounds the interpenetrations between ILO normativity and the political and legal specificities of member countries, notably through the incorporation of international norms into domestic legislation via the ratification of conventions, intervention at the level of political discourse, and complaints and claims against States submitted to the ILO. Analysis in this area brings out the interactions between the State, civil society, social partners, the administration of labour, and ILO political and normative influence. More specifically, it shows that all across the world the evolution of the systems of labour relations has been influenced by the ILO's way of doing things, as made evident by the legitimising effect derived from the normative standards set by it.

Although the ILO has had a significant impact throughout the world, its influence has not always been evident, given that it is often based on the dissemination of the organisation's ideas rather than on formal mechanisms aimed at an effective appropriation of its norms. At the symbolic level, the strength of the ILO is attested to by the fact that its norms have been naturalised both in the political arena and in the public space thanks to social actors in the area, whose activity is apparent in missions of technical support for the creation and revision of labour laws, in their mobilisation in support of labour struggles, and in the setting of a frame of reference to help political decision makers with regard to labour matters.

Hence the worldwide recognition of how important the ILO is for the world of work. In fact, thanks to its global agenda based on the issues of decent work, core labour standards, and the social role of globalisation in terms of shaping the systems governing national labour relations, social protection, and administration of labour, the ILO deserves credit for the international dissemination of the ideas that structure modern-day models of labour law and labour relations.

At a time when we hear calls for a broad discussion on the future of work and the ILO's future actions during its second century in the service of social justice, the pursuit of decent work needs to be given pride of place in the global, national and local strategies aimed at achieving economic and social progress. In a context in which transnational solutions for promoting fundamental rights at work are taking on an increasing role in terms of complementing national systems, and given the ILO's potential with regard to the defense of labour rights as they are attacked by the various strains of exceptionalism, austerity, flexibilisation and deregulation, it is imperative that its actions continue to encourage transnational dialogue, multilateralism and innovative political mobilisation towards the symbolic expansion of workers' rights as embodied in the principles of decent work, inclusion and social justice.

References

Henriques, Marina (2021), *O transconstitucionalismo de inclusão social da OIT e o caso português* (Doctoral thesis). Coimbra: Faculdade de Economia da Universidade de Coimbra.

International Labour Organisation (2020a), *World Employment and Social Outlook – Trends 2020*. Geneva: International Labour Office.

International Labour Organisation (2020b), *COVID-19 and the world of work: Impact and policy responses (1st Edition)*. Geneva: International Labour Office.

International Labour Organisation (2021), *ILO Monitor: COVID-19 and the world of work. Seventh edition*. Geneva: International Labour Office.

II.

LABOUR STANDARDS, JOBS AND CLIMATE CHALLENGES

CHAPTER 3:
TRADE, JOBS AND LABOUR STANDARDS[31]

Christian Viegelahn[32]

1. Introduction

In recent years, the distributive consequences of trade have come to the centre of global policy debates, often cited as one of the multiple factors behind the rise in populism and economic nationalism in some countries of the world (Rodrik, 2018). While there is a broad consensus on the overall economic gains of trade, not all subgroups of the population are always benefitting from the openness or the opening up to trade, and there have been experiences of job and income losses, as well as poor working conditions, in this context. In some instances, trade has been shown to cause adverse impacts (see, for example, Autor and Dorn, 2013). In other instances, events like the Rana Plaza garment factory collapse in Bangladesh

---

[31] This paper was received in July 2020 and corresponds to the participation in the seminar "International labour standards in trade agreements" (1st edition of "Cátedra OIT/ILO Chair"), held at the University of Coimbra, Faculty of Economics (FEUC), on April, 26, 2018. Any views expressed in this chapter are the personal views of the author and do not necessarily reflect the views of the International Labour Organization.

[32] Regional Office for Asia and the Pacific, Bangkok, International Labour Organization.

https://doi.org/10.14195/978-989-26-2277-4_5

in 2013, in which hundreds of workers died, have brought to light serious shortcomings with regard to labour standards in jobs related to trade and global-supply chains. Still, millions of workers and entrepreneurs worldwide base their livelihoods on trade, and the decent jobs and incomes that in many instances result from it.

COVID-19 is having an adverse impact on trade in a wide range of industries (ILO, 2020a). Millions of these jobs are now at risk due to the COVID-19 crisis. Estimates from the World Trade Organization (WTO) for the second quarter of 2020 suggest that merchandise trade has come down by 18.5% compared to the same quarter of the previous year. In a pessimistic scenario, trade in 2020 could even fall by 32% during the whole year, according to the WTO.[33] This sharp disruption followed a continuous upward trend, only interrupted by the global financial crisis in 2008-9. This massive collapse in trade during the ongoing COVID-19 crisis is mainly driven by two factors: the collapse of global consumer demand and the disruption of the supply of inputs into production across borders.

According to estimates of the International Labour Organization (ILO), as of 3 June 2020, 292 million jobs in manufacturing supply chains were at high risk due to the COVID-19-related drop in consumer demand suffering from reduced incomes, reduced working hours or unemployment (ILO, 2020b). Also the lack of key inputs has proved to be a serious obstacle for some enterprises with regard to maintaining production levels, with the manufacturing sector experiencing a disruption of imported input supply of on average up to 60%, observed in the beginning of April 2020.[34]

The ongoing disruptions are undoubtedly going to cause some long-term changes in the way global production is organised.

---

[33] See WTO website: https://www.wto.org/english/news_e/pres20_e/pr858_e.htm
[34] These are estimates for 64 countries, which cover 74% of the global labour force.

Some enterprises are likely to re-think their supply chains, in order to make them more resilient (Liao and Fan, 2020). The question of distributional consequences of trade and working conditions will remain highly relevant, especially in these circumstances, in which the ongoing changes related to the COVID-19 crisis are challenging conventional thinking. There are discussions about how the "new normal" in post-COVID-19 times is going to – and should – look like. According to the Director-General of the ILO, Guy Ryder, it is now *the time to look more closely at this new normal, and start on the task of making it a better normal, not so much for those who already have much, but for those who so obviously have too little* (ILO, 2020c).

As many challenges like climate change or the pandemic are truly global, multilateral institutions do have a role in shaping the new normal. Even though trade is closely linked to developments in the labour market, the issues of working conditions and labour standards are not subject to WTO committees or WTO treaties. The WTO's Ministerial Conference of 1996 in Singapore concluded with a commitment to adhere to internationally recognised core labour standards, but at the same time clearly referred to the ILO as a competent body that is supposed to set and deal with those standards. The Declaration also rejected the use of labour standards for protectionist purposes and vowed to continue the existing collaboration between WTO and ILO. The WTO's 2001 Ministerial Conference in Doha reaffirmed these commitments and definitions of mandates.

The ILO's mandate indeed covers the social and labour market impact of trade policies. Already the ILO Philadelphia Declaration of 1944 stated that it is the responsibility of the Organisation to examine and consider all international economic and financial policies and measures in light of the fundamental objective to achieve lasting peace and social justice. The ILO's Declaration on Fundamental Principles and Rights at Work of 1998 commits ILO members to respecting and enforcing core labour standards, regardless of whether or not they have ratified the relevant ILO Conventions. In addition, the Declaration stresses that these standards *should not be used for protectionist trade purposes*, and that the *comparative advantage of any country should in no way be called into question*.

The ILO's Declaration on Social Justice for a Fair Globalization of 2008 reaffirms ILO's mandate in an era of globalisation and comprehensively linked labour, economic and trade policies. In particular, it states that it is the ILO's mandate to evaluate the employment effects of trade policies, and confirms that the violation of Fundamental Principles and Rights at Work cannot be used as a legitimate comparative advantage. The Declaration also states that, upon request, the ILO can provide assistance to Members who aim to enhance decent work in the framework of bilateral or multilateral agreements.

Also the ILO Centenary Declaration, adopted in June 2019 at the International Labour Conference in Geneva and presenting a human-centred agenda for the future of work, makes reference to trade policies and the ILO's role in this context. It calls upon the ILO to *take an important role in the multilateral system, by reinforcing its cooperation and developing institutional arrangements with other organizations to promote policy coherence in pursuit of its human-centred approach to the future of work, recognizing the strong, complex and crucial links between social, trade, financial, economic and environmental policies*.

This chapter has two purposes.[35] First, it aims to provide an overview and discuss the impact of trade and trade policy on enterprises

---

[35] The chapter aims to summarise a special lecture given by the author at Coimbra University in April 2018, drawing on earlier research conducted by the ILO, as part

and their workers. Second, it explores whether labour provisions in trade agreements can be an entry point for stakeholders to discuss issues of decent work. Finally, the chapter explores the relationship between trade and jobs in the post-COVID-19 future, and aims to provide an outlook in this respect.

The next section in the chapter discusses recent trends in trade policy and its impact on enterprises and their workers. Section 3 presents labour provisions in trade agreements as a possible tool to enhance labour standards in the context of trade. The final section concludes by providing an outlook on trade and jobs in a Post-COVID-19 future.

2. Trade policy, enterprises and workers: what are the impacts?

Since the conclusion of the Uruguay round in 1994, the world has seen a standstill in multilateral trade negotiations at the WTO. Trade liberalisation in recent years has taken place through the conclusion of regional trade agreements of two or more trading partners. As of mid-2019, there were 293 of such agreements in force and notified to the WTO, a more than threefold increase since 2000 (ILO, 2019). Consequently, the simple average of the applied tariff rate across all goods has come down, driven by the conclusion of these trade agreements, from 10.8% in 2000, to 5.2% in 2017.[36] However, trade protection is still taking place in the form of non-tariff measures, including restrictions such as local content requirements, import licensing schemes, technical barriers to trade or contingent trade protection measures (Viegelahn, 2017).

Recent years have seen an upward trend in the use of trade protection, largely driven by measures that several G-20 countries

---

of its mandate on trade and labour.

[36] Data are taken from the World Bank data portal.

implemented, including measures taken as part of the so-called US-China trade war (Ernst et al, 2019). Tariffs imposed by the United States against imports from China have risen from a trade-weighted average of 3.1% in January 2018 to above 20% in January 2020. Similarly, tariffs imposed by China against imports from the United States have risen from 8.0 to more than 20% during the same period (Bown, 2020). According to the Global Trade Alert database, the number of import-related interventions that are discriminatory in nature and provide some countries with worse access to domestic markets has globally more than doubled between 2014 and 2019, providing some evidence for increasing trade protection.[37]

Both the introduction of trade barriers and the removal of trade barriers on foreign imports have an impact on enterprises and their workers, and it is important to understand these impacts in order to understand some of the distributive consequences of trade and trade policies (Viegelahn, 2017). It is important to point out that both the introduction and the removal of trade barriers are likely to have distributive consequences on enterprises and workers.

Trade liberalisation implemented in a country is likely to adversely impact import-competing enterprises in that country and their suppliers, which might be located in that same country or abroad. The removal of trade barriers exposes domestic import-competing enterprises to increased foreign import competition. This may in some cases cause the market exit of enterprises with related job dismissals; only the strongest companies will survive the competition. Also suppliers of import-competing enterprises will be adversely impacted and jobs are likely to be adversely impacted (Acemoglu et al, 2016). Conversely, trade protection has a positive impact on

---

[37] Also the COVID-19 crisis had an impact on trade policies, inducing some countries to impose export restrictions on goods like masks or hand sanitisers, in order to prevent domestic shortages.

import-competing enterprises, as it shields them from import competition, even though the impact has been shown to not always be uniformly positive for all enterprises (Konings and Vandenbussche, 2008). The effects on suppliers of these enterprises will also tend to be positive, as they will benefit from increased demand for intermediate inputs that they supply to import-competing enterprises.

Trade liberalisation is likely to have positive effects on domestic importers and their suppliers. Trade liberalisation provides firms with better access to foreign inputs, which is a key determinant of firm performance and can spur innovation (Shu and Steinwender, 2019). Access to foreign inputs provides opportunities to learn from new technologies, access to higher quality and also access to a wider variety of inputs that might not be available domestically. Also workers typically benefit when the enterprises that employ them have better access to foreign inputs (Amiti and Davis, 2012). Conversely, restricting the access to foreign inputs will adversely impact input-using enterprises and their workers (Vandenbussche and Viegelahn, 2018). Changes in the import tariff can also impact product market competition, as these changes affect only enterprises that import their input – i.e., they do not affect those that use domestic inputs.

Global supply chains are complex, with intermediate inputs crossing borders multiple times. The reliance on imported inputs makes enterprises dependent on trade policy choices by governments. Moreover, enterprises can be affected by trade policy in multiple ways, as one and the same enterprise can be an import-competing enterprise and an enterprise that uses imported inputs at the same time. The net effect of the introduction or removal of a trade barrier imposed on a certain good will hence crucially depend on the particular product the enterprise is selling and the particular input sourcing strategy of the enterprise.

Trade liberalisation or trade protection imposed by one country not only impacts enterprises and workers in that country, but also affects enterprises and their workers abroad. Trade liberalisation is likely to benefit foreign exporters and their suppliers. The removal of trade barriers provides foreign firms with increased export opportunities. The exported good becomes cheaper, which will increase demand. This can then increase the number of jobs that are dependent on these exports. This is also likely to have an impact on foreign exporters' suppliers, which will benefit from increased exports, as the increase in exports requires an increase in production which in turn increases the demand for inputs produced by suppliers.

Recent evidence points to substantial effects that tariffs can have on jobs in other countries. According to estimates, a reduction of the average goods tariff can be associated with an increase in the number of manufacturing jobs related to the trade flow that is covered by the tariff. It is also associated with an increase in the number of services jobs related to that trade flow, as service providers provide input into the production of manufacturing goods that are covered by the tariff (Kühn and Viegelahn, 2019).

Trade policy changes also impact on how and where firms set up their global production networks. Trade liberalisation can stimulate the creation of new jobs in global supply chains. It may incentivise lead firms to set up a supplier network that makes use of the free cross-border trade. Jobs created in foreign countries through these global production networks can play an important role in the development of these countries, as these jobs provide livelihood for millions of workers. However, there are documented cases of poor working conditions in global supply chains, including violations of occupational safety and health standards, low wages, excessive and volatile working hours or child labour (see e.g. ILO, OECD, IOM and UNICEF, 2019).

There are multiple factors that affect the quality of jobs in global supply chains. First, the bargaining power of supplier enterprises vis-à-vis lead enterprises can have an impact. When supplier enterprises have more bargaining power and are able to negotiate better contracts with lead enterprises, they will in general be able to provide their workers with better pay and better working conditions. The bargaining power in turn is affected by the complexity of the task that the supplier is asked to carry out for the lead enterprise. If the task is less complex and could be easily carried out by other suppliers, the bargaining power will be low. If in contrast the task is more complex, then it will be less straightforward for the lead enterprises to find another supplier, which gives more bargaining power to the supplier firm. A supplier's bargaining power is also affected by the number of lead enterprises in the market. If suppliers have the option to supply their inputs to other lead enterprises, this will raise their bargaining power, compared to the situation in which there is only one or few lead enterprises in the market. Finally, the particularities of the sector in which lead enterprises are operating can also have an impact on working conditions in supplier enterprises. If the lead firms has requirements to produce in a flexible manner, then this can have an adverse impact on working conditions in supplier firms, which in a response need to work with more flexible contracts.

Another factor that impacts the quality of jobs in global supply chains is the extent to which the country in which factories are located adheres to international labour standards and has effective and well-resourced labour inspection systems in place, which can ensure compliance with international labour standards by supplier enterprises. Third, social dialogue and the respect for the right to organise is an important factor that determines the quality of jobs, as a well-functioning social dialogue can lead to higher compliance with labour standards. A fourth contributor to decent work conditions in global supply chains are corporate social responsibility (CSR) initiatives, in which lead and supplier enterprises commit to good labour practices. A fifth factor that can contribute to the quality of jobs in global supply chains is consumer awareness and behaviour. Reputational risks related to poor-quality jobs in global supply chains may incentivise lead enterprises to exercise supply chain due diligence. Finally, there is also the role of labour market policies and institutions in contributing to the prevalence of high quality jobs in global supply chains.

Recent global policy initiatives such as the Vision Zero Fund (VZF) initiative provide an example of what the way forward could look like. The VZF is a G7-initiated multilateral fund, endorsed by G20 countries and financed through contributions from governments, international organisations, NGOs or private sources. The purpose of the VZF is to prevent work-related deaths, injuries and diseases in global supply chains. Other efforts to improve working conditions in global supply chains include the Resolution concerning decent work in GSCs, adopted at the International Labour Conference in June 2016, as well as the Revised MNE Declaration, adopted in March 2017.

The ILO Tripartite Meeting of Experts to Promote Decent Work and Protection of Fundamental Principles and Rights at Work for Workers in Export Processing Zones (EPZs) concluded, in November 2017, that "all companies have a responsibility to respect workers' rights and use their leverage to take steps to ensure that the rights of workers in their supply chains are also respected and that workers have access to remedy when their rights are violated".

Besides these multilateral initiatives, national policy action is required. While there are overall gains from trade, this does not imply that everyone gains from trade. Labour market policies and institutions can contribute to more inclusive and sustainable trade, including employment protection, minimum wage legislation, social protection floors and systems, as well as training policies. Workers can participate in gains from trade, in particular when they can engage in collective bargaining, are free to associate and have an active social dialogue with employers.

The COVID-19 crisis will likely cause enterprises to re-think their supply chains, in order to increase their resilience (ILO, 2020b). The solutions that will be found should also aim to contribute to achieving decent work in global supply chains, in order to pave the path for a sustainable and inclusive recovery from this crisis and a "new normal" that is a "better normal".

3. Can labour provisions in trade agreements be a possible tool?

Labour provisions in trade agreements can potentially provide an entry point for stakeholders to discuss issues related to decent jobs in global supply chains (Viegelahn, 2017). Over time, many countries have increasingly used labour provisions in trade agreements that they conclude, to provide a framework for decent work in the context of trade. Such labour provisions provide an entry point for stakeholders to discuss issues related to labour standards and the distributional effects of trade. According to ILO (2016), labour provisions can be defined as *any standard which addresses labour relations or minimum working terms or conditions, mechanisms for monitoring or promoting compliance, and/or a framework for cooperation*. This definition groups together a broad range of labour provisions. There is a dual focus of trade-related labour provisions. There is a governance focus, through references to labour commitments or details on compliance mechanisms. More than two thirds of all labour provisions that form part of trade agreements concluded so far, have made reference to ILO instruments such as the 1998 ILO Declaration on Fundamental Principles and Rights at Work or the ILO fundamental Conventions (ILO, 2019). There is also a focus on cooperation, with the mentioning of cooperative activities and dialogue and the monitoring of labour issues. Labour provisions can include either one or both of these elements.

The use of labour provisions in trade agreements has become more and more common over the past years. Out of 293 trade agreements in force as of mid-2019, 85 trade agreements included labour provisions (ILO, 2019). The European Union, the United States and Canada have traditionally been major actors when it comes to including labour provisions in trade agreements. However, some new actors have also emerged, such as Chile and New Zealand. Also an increasing number of South-South trade agreements include labour provisions.

There have been concerns that labour provisions would have an adverse impact on trade, partially due to their potential association with additional costs for firms needing to comply with labour standards. There is no evidence that labour provisions in trade agreements divert or decrease trade flows. Trade agreements both with and without labour provisions have been shown to have a positive impact on trade to a similar extent. Trade agreements with labour provisions, which came into force between 1995 and 2014, have on average increased trade by 28%, which compares with 26% for trade agreements without labour provisions (ILO, 2016). The two impacts are not significantly different from each other in a statistical sense. These results have been confirmed by further research (Carrère et al, 2017), which found either no impact or not even a positive impact of labour provisions on trade, when focusing on exports from low- to high-income countries.

In some recent attempts to evaluate the effectiveness of labour provisions in trade agreements with regard to their contribution towards decent work outcomes, empirical evidence points to higher labour force participation rates, especially among women. Countries that conclude trade agreements with labour provisions have a more favourable trend in labour force participation rates, after concluding such an agreement, than countries that conclude trade agreements without such labour provisions. Furthermore, the gender gap in labour force participation rates is estimated to decrease on average by 1.1 percentage points, following the conclusion of a trade agreement with labour provisions (ILO, 2016). One driver of this finding could be the increased reference to gender-related issues within labour provisions in trade agreements. This includes references to Convention No. 100 on Equal Remuneration and Convention No. 111 on Discrimination (Employment and Occupation), which are both recognised as fundamental Conventions.

There is also country case study evidence that points to the potential of labour provisions to lead to more equal labour market outcomes for women and men. The Cambodia-United States Bilateral Textile Agreement, which combined economic incentives with the obligation for textile manufacturers to comply with core labour standards, led to a statistically significant reduction in the gender wage gap in the Cambodian textile sector (López Mourelo and Samaan, 2017). The monitoring of compliance with core labour standards at the enterprise-level is likely to have played an important role in this outcome (ILO, 2016).

The key mechanism through which labour provisions in trade agreements have an impact is through labour market institutions, supported by stakeholder involvement (ILO, 2016). Labour provisions that have been successful in the sense that they can be linked to better decent work outcomes, all have in common the fact that a wide range of stakeholders, including social partners, were involved in the negotiation phase. A combination of mechanisms has been effective, with synergies between these mechanisms. This includes a legal mechanism whereby parties can file submissions to activate the dispute settlement mechanism and provide their views during dispute settlement. It includes a political mechanism, with participation of stakeholders in congress or parliament hearings and public awareness raising. It includes an economic mechanism, which works through the reputational risk of States and businesses. It includes a technical cooperation and dialogue mechanism, with the organisation of public conferences – in which social partners participate –, trainings, agreements for technical assistance, and dialogue. Finally, it includes a monitoring mechanism, which can take place through stakeholder advisory bodies or other mechanisms outside of the agreements. In this context, cross-border coalitions of civil society organisations can also play an important role.

4. Conclusion

The distributional impacts of trade and working conditions in jobs linked to trade and global supply chains are important factors in a free and fair trading system, which contributes to sustainable and inclusive economic growth. This chapter described some aspects of the distributional impact of trade policies and presented labour provisions in trade agreements as one possible entry point for stakeholders to discuss these issues. The promotion of social dialogue to discuss any trade-related challenges is important to make sure that the interests of both workers and enterprises as key stakeholders are being considered in any trade-related government decisions. Labour market policies and institutions, including well-functioning labour inspection systems and corporate social responsibility, are important to ensure that trade is ultimately beneficial for all.

The world is currently being hit by the COVID-19 crisis, with workers and enterprises being faced with severe challenges and hardships around the globe. It will be important for governments to pursue the goal of "building back better", based on the human-centred agenda for the future of work as outlined in the ILO Centenary Declaration (ILO, 2020d). The integration of trade-related objectives with social or environmental objectives will also be key, to ensure policy coherence and to ensure that trade contributes to economic growth that is sustainable and inclusive. The multilateral system has an important role to play in highlighting the linkages of trade policies with social and environmental objectives and in ensuring policy coherence, in order to create a "new normal" that is also a "better normal".

References

Acemoglu, D.; Autor, D.; Dorn, D.; Hanson, G.H.; Price, B. (2016), "Import competition and the great US employment sag of the 2000s", in *Journal of Labor Economics* Vol. 34 (S1 Part 2), pp. S141-S198.

Amiti, M.; Davis, D.R. (2012), "Trade, firms and wages: Theory and evidence", in *Review of Economic Studies* Vol. 79 (1), pp. 1-36.

Autor, D.H.; Dorn, D. (2013), "The China syndrome: Local labour market effects of import competition in the United States", in *American Economic Review* Vol. 103(6), pp. 2121-68.

Bown, C. (2020), "US-China trade war tariffs: An up-to-date chart", Peterson Institute for International Economics, available at: https://www.piie.com/research/piie-charts/us-china-trade-war-tariffs-date-chart [2 July 2020].

Carrère, C.; Olarreaga, M.; Raess, D. (2017), *Labor clauses in trade agreements: Worker protection or protectionism?*, CEPR Discussion Paper No. DP12251, London: Centre for Economic Policy Research.

Ernst, E; Merola, R.; Samaan, D. (2019), *Trade wars and their labour market effects*, Research Department Working Paper No. 48, International Labour Organization: Geneva.

International Labour Organization (2016), *Assessment of labour provisions in trade and investment arrangements*, Geneva.

International Labour Organization (2019), *Labour provisions in G7 trade agreements: A comparative perspective*, Geneva.

International Labour Organization (2020a), The effects of *Covid-19 on trade and global supply chains*, ILO Research Brief, Geneva.

International Labour Organization (2020b), *Covid-19 and global supply chains: How the jobs crisis propagates across borders*, ILO Policy Brief, Geneva.

International Labour Organization (2020c), *New normal? Better normal!*, Op-ed by Director-General Guy Ryder, 1 May 2020, Geneva.

International Labour Organization (2020d), *ILO Monitor: Covid-19 and the world of work. Fifth edition. Updated estimates and analysis*, Geneva.

International Labour Organization; Organization for Economic Co-operation and Development (OECD); International Organization for Migration (IOM); United Nation's International Children's Fund (UNICEF) (2019), *Ending child labour, forced labour and human trafficking in global supply chains*, Geneva.

Konings, J.; Vandenbussche, H. (2008), "Heterogeneous responses of firms to trade protection", in *Journal of International Economics* Vol. 76 (2), pp. 371-83.

Kühn, S. and Viegelahn C. (2019), "Foreign trade barriers and jobs in global supply chains", in *International Labour Review* Vol. 158 (1), pp. 137-67.

Liao, R.; Fan, Z. (2020), *Supply chains have been upended. Here's how to make them more resilient*, Geneva: World Economic Forum.

López Mourelo, E.; Samaan, D. (2017), "Can labour provisions in trade agreements promote gender equality? Empirical evidence from Cambodia", in *Review of Development Economics* Vol. 22 (1), pp. 404-33.

Rodrik, D. (2018), "Populism and the economics of globalization", in *Journal of International Business Policy* Vol. 1, pp. 12-33.

Shu, P.; Steinwender, C. (2019), "The impact of trade liberalization on firm productivity and innovation", in *Innovation Policy and the Economy* Vol. 19 (1), pp. 39-68.

Vandenbussche, H.; Viegelahn, C. (2018), "Input reallocation within multi-product firms", in *Journal of International Economics* Vol. 114, pp. 63-79.

Viegelahn, C. (2017), "How trade policy affects firms and workers in global supply chains: an overview", Chapter 13, in *Handbook on Assessment of Labour Provisions in Trade and Investment Arrangements*, Geneva: International Labour Office.

COMMENT:
TRADE AND SOCIAL RESPONSIBILITY IN A POST-COVID 19 WORLD

Susana Garrido[38] and André Saramago[39]

This essay is a reflection on the main ideas developed in the chapter entitled "Trade, jobs and labour standards", by Christian Viegelahn.

Trade represents an important economic activity, one that contributes to the growth of employment and consequently to the wealth of countries. It is true that not all subgroups of population benefit from this activity and some of the problems raised by the author are indeed part of the reality in many countries, but some of them are structural, that is, they already exist independently of an open market. Many companies in less developed countries do not respect either labour rights regarding, for example, the working conditions of employees and health and safety at work, or fair operating practices regarding competition, respect for property rights, corruption, political involvement or promotion of social responsibility across the supply chains (ISO 26000).

It is widely recognised that large global companies from more developed countries are always trying to take advantage of their

---

[38] University of Coimbra, Faculty of Economics, Centre for Business and Economics Research.

[39] University of Coimbra, Faculty of Economics, Centre for Social Studies.

https://doi.org/10.14195/978-989-26-2277-4_6

higher bargaining power by pressing small companies in less developed countries to accept highly disadvantageous trade conditions, and this further contributes to the degradation of the labour market in those countries. However, this scenario is changing because of some global companies that, in an attempt to improve their image and reputation, and also in order to obtain Corporation B Certification, are becoming more committed to socially responsible practices in engaging not only with their employees but also with their stakeholders.

This occurs also in response to the growth of movements, both in the Global North and the Global South, that seek to reinforce corporate responsibility by appealing to fair trade and to the need to compensate for the uneven, and sometimes negative, impacts of free trade in less developed countries.

However, these developments, and the ways in which they sought to contribute to the quality of life of "millions of workers and entrepreneurs worldwide [who] base their livelihoods on trade, and the decent jobs and incomes that in many instances result from it" were deeply altered by the COVID-19 pandemic, which led to a global collapse of consumer demand and disruption of global supply networks. Consumer demand dropped to levels never seen before. It decreased by 11 to 26% in China, USA and Western Europe, mainly because of cutbacks in in-person services, which in turn had a direct impact in terms of loss of jobs.

The COVID-19 pandemic thus led to a global disruption of labour markets during 2020, with millions of people losing their jobs, and others quickly having to adjust to working from home, with several implications at the level of mental health and work/family life balance. Many other workers were considered indispensable and continued to work in strategic activities, such as hospitals and grocery stores, on garbage management and in warehouses, but under new health protocols to reduce the spread of the novel virus.

Before COVID-19, the largest disruptions to work involved new technologies and growing trade links (supply chains working on a global scale). COVID-19 has, for the first time, called attention to the importance of the physical dimension of work, especially in those cases in which physical proximity was considered critical: such as medical care, personal care, on-site customer service, leisure and travel. However, and because of the pandemic context, some of the jobs in these areas migrated to e-commerce and other digital transactions, a change in behaviour that is likely to continue.

Perhaps the most obvious impact of COVID-19 on the labour force has been the dramatic increase in employees working remotely. In this context, the question that is raised all over the world is whether remote work might persist after the pandemic and, if so, what will be its main consequences? According to the consulting company McKinsey, the CEOs of the big companies plan to reduce office spaces by 30%, which could result in a decrease on demand for restaurants and retail in downtown areas, as well as for public transportation. Also, many consumers discovered the convenience of e-commerce during the pandemic, contributing to its growth by two to five times the rate before COVID-19.

Moreover, the shift to digital transactions was an important driver of job profiles. The expansion of e-commerce has forced growth in delivery, transportation, and warehouse jobs. This was very visible in China, where e-commerce, delivery, and social media jobs grew by more than 5.1 million during the first half of 2020.

Before the COVID-19 pandemic, and because of the fourth/fifth Industrial revolution, the topic of new challenges to the labour market was already under discussion, with the following factors being identified as the main drivers of changes in jobs: automation, rising incomes, aging population, increased use of technology, climate change, rising education levels, etc. With the addition COVID-19, we have also the following: accelerating automation, accelerated e-commerce, increased remote work, and reduced business travel.

A post-COVID-19 scenario projected by the prestigious consulting firm, McKinsey & Company, in an attempt to delineate the evolution of employment until 2030, identified the occupational categories most likely to show marked growth. These included health aides, techs; care workers; STEM (Science, Technology, Engineering and Maths) professionals and health professionals. On the other hand, the following occupational categories will face a decline: office support; production and warehousing; agriculture; customer service and sales (Figure 1).

Figure 1 – Changes in occupational categories by 2030 in post-COVID-19 scenario

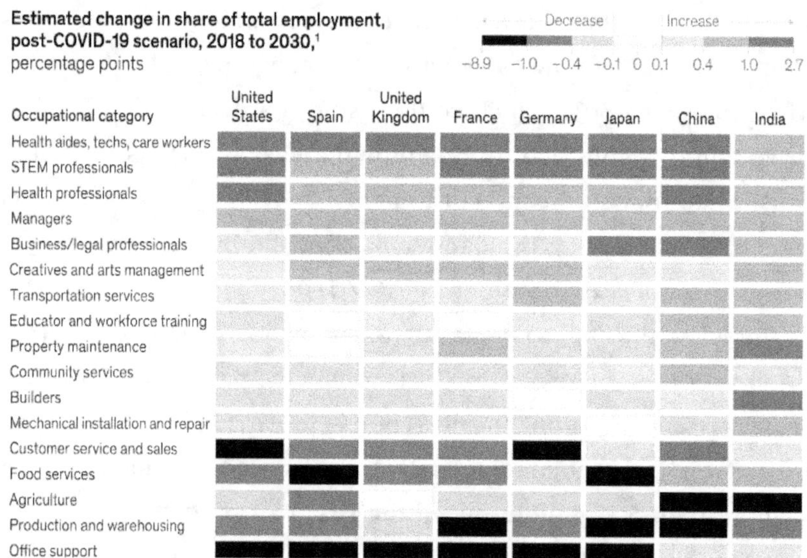

Source: McKinsey Global Institute analysis (2022), "The future of work after Covid-19", https://www. mckinsey.com/featured-insights/future-of-work/the- -future-of-work-after-covid-19 [accessed on Febrary, 3rd, 2022]

Another topic addressed by Christian Viegelahn is the lack of raw materials, which "has proved to be a serious obstacle for some enterprises in maintaining their production, with the manufacturing sector experiencing a disruption of imported input supply on average up to 60%, observed in the beginning of April 2020".

It is true that raw materials are crucial to produce a broad range of goods used in everyday life. They are present in all kinds of industries and across the entire supply chain, are considered strategic for the strength of the industrial base of any country, and contribute to increasing its growth and competitiveness.

The over-production and over-consumption that characterise the global economy derive from a linear economic model (this means that raw materials are used to make a product, and that after that use any waste is thrown away) and have given rise to accelerating cycles of technological innovation. Moreover, the rapid growth of emerging economies has also led to a steady increase in demand for metals and minerals.

However, this economic model has increasingly demonstrated its limits and fundamental incompatibility with the sustainability of the natural processes on which life on the planet depends. According to the European Environmental Agency, the per capita consumption of energy and materials is respectively three times and two times greater than that consumed in 1900. Moreover, there are now over 7.2 billion individuals sustained by these resources, compared with 1.6 billion in 1900. Another important and concerning fact is that humans are consuming more resources than the Earth can regenerate. A paradigm shift towards a more circular and regenerative economy, in line with the sustainable development goals defined in Agenda 2030, has thus become imperative. This urgent paradigm shift towards a circular economic system should be achieved through the maximisation of reuse, repair, remanufacturing and recycling to create a closed-loop system, minimising not only the use of resources input but also the creation of waste.

The challenges of climate change, the breakdown of ecosystems or COVID-19 are very serious, have a transnational character and need to be addressed synergically at a country, continental, and global level. That is, the world as a whole should be engaged on finding solutions to mitigate all the negative impacts derived from these problems. The COVID-19 pandemic is the first genuinely global health emergency with which our planet is faced, even if with highly uneven impacts across countries and regions. Both in itself, and when combined with the global ecological crisis, it highlights the fragility of global stability and institutions.

In order to address these challenges and build a set of local, national and global institutions capable of supervising a recovery process from the COVID-19 pandemic that is consistent with the needs of human individuals and the planet as a whole, both individual companies and supply chains need to reinforce their commitment to the principles of Corporate Social Responsibility (CSR) and to more socially and ecologically responsible behaviour. These principles are: accountability, transparency, ethical behaviour, respect for the interests of stakeholders, respect for the rule of law, respect for international norms of behaviour and respect for human rights. Beyond these principles, it is also important that a set of issues related to the following organisational dimensions of governance be addressed: human rights, labour practices, the environment, fair operating practices, consumer issues, and community involvement and development. It is important that organisations and the corresponding supply chains follow the guidelines suggested by the International Standard for Social Responsibility, (ISO 26000), in order to change their behaviour. Furthermore, the compliance of individual companies and supply chains with CSR also depends fundamentally on the capacity of states and international institutions to ensure the required supervision and respect for guidelines.

CHAPTER 4:
SHOULD JOBS CARE ABOUT THE ENVIRONMENT?[40]

Guillermo Montt[41]

Climate change and other forms of environmental degradation are among the defining challenges of our time. Humanity is using 1.7 times more resources and producing more waste than the planet can regenerate and absorb. We are using tomorrow's resources to satisfy today's needs (Global Footprint Network, 2017). Humanity's influence on the Earth system, which has been accelerating since the 1950s, has led to unprecedented rates of biodiversity loss, the emission of novel entities, damage to the ozone layer, soil degradation and changes to global biogeochemical flows, and has altered the Earth system on a worldwide, and in certain cases irreversible, scale (Steffen, Broadgate et al., 2015; Steffen, Richardson et al., 2015). Environmental damage is a feature of our present. Its likely continuation will define our future and, in particular, the future of work.

---

[40] This paper was received in June 2020 and corresponds to the participation in the seminar "International labour standards in trade agreements" (1st edition of "Cátedra OIT/ILO Chair"), held at the University of Coimbra, Faculty of Economics (FEUC), on February 22, 2018.

[41] Social Protection Specialist at the International Labour Office. Up to 2019, his work centred on the relationship between decent work and environmental sustainability, the subject of ILO's 2018 thematic edition of the World Employment and Social Outlook report. He holds a PhD in Sociology from the University of Notre Dame (USA).

https://doi.org/10.14195/978-989-26-2277-4_7

Several examples show the deterioration of the Earth ecosystem's sourcing functions or the generation of waste beyond the Earth's sink function. Deterioration negatively impacts future economic activity and the future of work. When it comes to producing resources (sourcing capacity), at least 31% of the world's marine fisheries are exploited beyond their capacity to replenish stock (FAO, 2016; Pauly and Zeller, 2016), about a third of the world's soils are degraded and, if current trends continue, all of the world's soils may be degraded in 60 years (FAO, 2015). Regarding the capacity of the Earth to absorb waste (sink capacity), climate change is the result of both the generation of waste in the form of greenhouse gas (GHG) emissions beyond the Earth's capacity to sequester and a reduction in the Earth's sink functions through, for example, land use change (IPCC, 2013). The release of pollutants beyond the capacity of the ecosystem to absorb them affects the quality of soils, water and air, in turn damaging the ecosystems' ability to perform their source functions.

To a large extent, this is driven by a development model that uses more natural resources that the planet creates and generates more waste than the planet can absorb. Such is the case of the world as a whole, and Portugal in particular (Global Footprint Network, 2017). Development paths are closely intertwined with the use of more resources and the generation of more waste. Comparing countries' Human Development Index with the use of resources and the generation of waste together illustrates this idea. Ideally, we would see many countries that are able to combine high human development with a low environmental footprint, yet this is rarely the case. The majority of countries have either high development and a high footprint (as would be the case for Portugal) or low development and a consequent low footprint. Two countries escaped this trend in 2013: Sri Lanka and the Dominican Republic, but by 2014 their status had already changed.

Several questions arise from these facts and from the need to redirect development paths towards environmental sustainability. First, and given that environmental degradation will continue to be a feature of our future, should the world of work be concerned about environmental degradation? (the answer is yes). Second, is economic growth and environmental sustainability compatible with more and more decent work? (the answer is also yes). And third, what would these environmentally sustainable, decent-work promoting economies look like?

First: Why should the world of work care about environmental degradation?

For one, many jobs depend on scarce and finite natural resources. The economic activity of many countries, and the jobs that depend on them, remain coupled to the extraction of natural resources. In 2015, for example, 1.7% of global GDP came from natural resource rents, but this share reached 21% in the Arab States and 7.1% in Africa. Natural resource rents accounted for more than 10% of national GDP in 40 countries, 25 of which are in Africa and six in the Arab States (World Bank, 2017). This means that jobs in agriculture, fishing and forestry (and those that depend indirectly on these sectors) will be hard hit by the unsustainable exploitation of soil and water and of marine and forest resources.

Second: Economic activity, and jobs, depend on ecosystem services.

Ecosystem services are processes or goods produced naturally by ecosystems that have a human value. They range from forests' capacity to produce wood, purify the air, regulate rain patterns, regulate and purify water flows to ocean ecosystems' capacity to replenish fish. For example, dry-land farming relies on rain for irrigation and farmers rely on forests to prevent floods; farmers also rely on the capacity of the soil to maintain and renew its nutrients and the wind and insects to pollinate plants. Most of the activity in industries like agriculture, forestry, fishing, food, beverages and tobacco, wood and paper, renewable energy, water supply depend on biodiversity and ecosystem services. The textile, chemicals and tourism industries also depend, at least in part, on ecosystem services. Throughout these industries, ecosystems generate value, services and goods – including the provision of genetic resources, fresh water –, pollinate, disperse seeds, produce fibers and generate educational, aesthetic and cultural value.

I mentioned earlier that 31% of fisheries are being exploited beyond their capacity to replenish stock. Sardine fisheries in Portugal are quickly reaching this threshold. If all fisheries were to collapse (a possible scenario in the coming 50 years), 45 million jobs in fisheries would be lost, as well as the jobs throughout the value chain that produce for the fisheries and trade and add value to their goods. We estimate these direct and indirect jobs losses at more than 80 million.

In all, around 1.2 billion jobs worldwide depend directly on ecosystem services, a large majority of them in the agricultural sector.

Third: Economic activity relies on a stable, disaster-free environment

Environmental degradation also produces risks that affect economic activity and jobs. Risks can stem from slow-onset events (as is the case with droughts, erosion, soil degradation or sea-level rise) or rapid-onset events (as is the case with extreme weather events), and can be local or global. Environmental risks can result from human activity (e.g. water pollution from non-compliant industrial activity) or natural hazards (e.g. water pollution following a volcanic eruption). Human activity can also increase the occurrence and intensity of natural hazards (e.g. increasing the intensity and frequency of extreme weather events resulting from human-induced climate change) and their consequences (for example, mangrove deforestation increases the consequences of storms on shores).

Soil, air and water pollution alone led to nine million deaths in 2015. Taking into account only premature deaths, air pollution costs the world economy about US$225 billion in lost labour income and US$5 trillion in welfare losses. The detrimental effect of air pollution reduces productivity and working hours through the deterioration of the health of workers themselves, and of women when they take the burden of the caregiving role for sick children. Air pollution thus increases gender inequality in the labour market.

As a result of climate change and other forms of environmental degradation, projections point towards an increase in the frequency and intensity of extreme weather events and disasters (IPCC, 2014). With each disaster, jobs and productivity are lost. Between 2000 and 2015, 23 million working-life years were lost annually resulting from different environmentally-related hazards caused or enhanced by human activity. Beyond accounts of untold human suffering, this is equivalent to 0.8% of a year's work, considering that 2.8 billion people aged 15 to 64 are in employment in any given year.

Rising temperatures increase the incidence of heat stress and health risks, and the proportion of working hours during which a worker needs to rest and cool down the body to maintain the core body temperature below 38°C and avoid heat stroke. During the course of the century, and as a result of human-induced climate change, many of the more than four billion people who live in hot areas will experience negative health and safety effects and reduced work capacity. Agricultural workers will be the worst affected, in view of the physical nature of their work – it being undertaken outside – and of the fact that a large number of workers are engaged in agriculture in the areas most affected by future high temperatures. Even greater temperature rises, as predicted under a business-as-usual scenario, will make some of these areas unproductive, displacing a large number of workers.

Fourth: Environmental degradation enhances inequality

People who are marginalised socially, economically, culturally, politically, institutionally or in any other way are especially vulnerable to the effects of climate change and other forms of environmental degradation. Environmental degradation thus increases inequality. People in poverty are generally more exposed to the effects of hazards and disasters, as it is more difficult for them to access resources to adapt to climate change, including land, credit, agricultural inputs, participation in decision-making bodies, access to technology, social insurance and training. Also, indigenous and tribal peoples and the rural poor are especially vulnerable to environmental degradation that limits the provision of ecosystem services. In general, inadequate social protection systems limit people's capacity to adapt to the immediate effects of environmental hazards and disasters on income security, with informal workers becoming a specific vulnerable group as well.

Exposure and vulnerability to environmental risks are not evenly distributed across countries; indeed, 80% of the total life years lost to disasters are spread across low- and middle-income countries. Poor and low-income countries are at higher risk in view of their lower capacity to mitigate the damage and mobilise resources for reconstruction. For example, climate change is a direct threat to poverty eradication, because it causes changes in ecosystems which in turn affect food prices and security and lead to more extreme and more frequent natural hazards and the magnification of health threats, a key source of chronic poverty. Gender differences in social and economic roles and responsibilities exacerbate the vulnerability of women. For the majority of women working in the informal economy, in small enterprises and with more difficult access to adaptation resources (land, credit, technology, etc.), it is particularly difficult to recover from the effects of environmental disasters.

These four channels highlight how environmental degradation threatens the world of work and how advancing environmental sustainability is necessary to promote the sustainability of jobs, work and development. A transition towards environmentally sustainable economies is required to advance social justice. This transition involves a structural transformation that touches all sectors, but is led by changes in agriculture, fisheries, forestry, manufacturing, waste management, buildings and construction and transportation.

Modelling the employment effects of a transition

We modelled what a transition in the energy sector would entail for the world of work. The Paris Agreement's commitment to limiting global warming to under 2 degrees would limit the likelihood of catastrophic and irreversible climate change. This goal could be achieved by a transition in the energy sector through a structural shift away from fossil fuels and towards renewable energy sources (e.g. solar, wind, geothermal), as well as investment in energy efficiency (e.g. building retrofitting, to require less energy to control the internal temperature of buildings). We simulated what these changes would mean in terms of total employment through multi-regional input-

-output tables to account for the economic linkages across industries and national borders. Advancing towards the decarbonisation of the energy sector will result in the net creation of 18 million jobs around the world. This is the result of 24 million jobs created and 6 million jobs destroyed. The Americas, Asia and the Pacific and Europe would see a net job creation of 3, 15 and 2 million net jobs created, respectively. Both Africa and the Middle East are expected to lose about 300,000 jobs each between now and 2050 if the economic structure of these regions does not divert from current trends.

The construction and the renewable energy sectors lead job creation with around 6 million and 2.5 million jobs, respectively. This is expected, given the importance of energy efficiency and renewables in a scenario of energy sustainability. Industries that supply inputs to these industries, which are not necessarily sustainable in terms of resource or energy intensity, will also see job creation, as is the case with the manufacturing of electrical parts and machinery and the mining of copper ores and concentrates. These two sectors will see job creation, with around 2.5 and 1.2 million jobs, respectively. Job losses are concentrated in petroleum refining (around 1.6 million), crude petroleum extraction (around 1.4 million), production of electricity by coal (around 0.8) and the mining of coal (around 0.7). Of the 163 industries analysed, only 14 see employment losses of more than 10,000 jobs. The concentration of employment loss in a few industries is due to the fact that reaching the 2°C goal requires the downsizing of a few carbon-intensive industries which are, in general, very capital-intensive and source input from other capital intensive industries; a large percentage reduction in output in these industries leads to comparatively small reductions in employment.

We also modelled what a more resource-efficient economy would look like. Indeed, resource-intensive sectors such as mining and manufacturing will also undergo substantial changes on the path towards sustainability. The current economic model of production of goods could be typified as linear: extract, manufacture, use and discard. The circular economy, as an alternative, is based on the principle of produce-service-use-reuse. One of its tenets is to reduce the extraction of raw materials and to rely instead on reuse, repair and recycling. In a circular economy, products are designed to have longer lives and to be repaired, reused or recycled to the extent possible, as certain materials can be recycled more times (e.g. metals) than others (e.g. paper). Through changes to the incentive structure for enterprises to produce more durable goods, and goods that serve as inputs into other production streams when they are no longer usable, the circular economy keeps products, components and materials at a high level of utility. It maximises product life and promotes the reuse, refurbishment, remanufacture and recycling of inputs and components. In view of the interlinkages in the manufacturing sector and the fact that material inputs are recycled or reused, employment changes are warranted in manufacturing, extractive and waste management industries. A circular economy also results in changes in the services sector, as repair and rental services gain in importance over the replacement and ownership of goods.

We model the employment impact of a sustained 5% annual increase in recycling rates for plastics, glass, wood pulp, metals and minerals, replacing the direct extraction of the primary resources for these products. This scenario also models growth in the service economy, which, through rental and repair services, reduces the private ownership and replacement of goods at an annual rate of 1%. Under this scenario, worldwide employment would grow to be, in 2030, 0.1% higher than a business-as-usual scenario. This is equivalent to a net job creation of around six million more jobs. The biggest change, however, is a reallocation of production. Employment growth is led by growth in services and waste management, with some 50 and 45 million jobs, respectively. Overall employment gains offset employment losses in mining and manufacturing (where losses are expected to be around 50 and 60 million jobs, respectively). This important reallocation is largely due to the replacement of the extraction of primary resources and the production of metals, plastics, glass and pulp by the recycling and reprocessing of secondary metals, plastics, glass and pulp. This global sectoral reallocation leads to different effects in the various regions. Like the energy scenario, net employment growth should be expected in the Americas (over 10 million jobs) and Europe (around 0.5 million jobs) and losses expected in Africa (around one million jobs) and the Middle East (around 200,000 jobs). In Asia and the Pacific, the circular economy is expected to bring employment losses as well (around five million jobs). Employment losses are expected only if no action is taken to promote economic diversification. By benefiting jobs in services, and if the gender distribution across sectors remains similar, the circular economy will raise both the female share of employment and the share of highly skilled jobs. However, it will also result in a small increase in the numbers of own-account and contributing family workers, highlighting the importance of decent work policies to complement policies to promote the circular economy. As employment will grow in the waste management sector, special attention is required to ensure that the new jobs in these sectors are decent.

Brief policy implications

Several policy measures are needed to advance this transition towards environmentally sustainable economies and to ensure that it leads to more and better jobs. They include a strong and coherent legal framework that simultaneously promotes decent work and environmental sustainability, social protection to protect workers who may lose out from this transition, skills development to ensure that workers have the skills to fill the new jobs that will appear in a green economy, facilitate social dialogue as it offers an opportunity to build the needed consensus and seek solutions and create the mechanisms to guarantee the rights of workers, communities and vulnerable groups' rights.

Further reading

ILO (2018), *World employment outlook 2018: Greening with Jobs*. Geneva: International Labour Office.

ILO (2019a), *Working on a warmer planet: The impact of heat stress on labour productivity and decent work*. Geneva: International Labour Office.

ILO (2019b), *Skills for a greener future: A global view*. Geneva: International Labour Office.

ILO and UNECE (2020), *Jobs in green and healthy transport: Making the green shift*. Geneva: United Nations Commission for Europe.

Montt, G., Harsdorff, M. and Fraga, F. (2018), "The future of work in a changing natural environment: Climate change, degradation and sustainability". *The Future of Work Research Paper Series*, No. 4 (Geneva).

Montt, G., Wiebe, K., Harsdorff, M., Simas, M., Bonnet, A., Wood, R. (2018), "Does climate action destroy jobs? An assessment of the employment implications of the 2-degree goal", *International Labour Review*, Vol. 157, No. 4, 519-556.

THE WORLD OF WORK AND THE ENVIRONMENT: WHAT CAN WE EXPECT AND HOW CAN WE INFLUENCE OUR FUTURE?

Luís Cruz[42] and Eduardo Barata[43]

"Climate change and other forms of environmental degradation are among the defining challenges of our time" (Guillermo Montt). And this issue cannot any longer be addressed as an environmental problem only, but should be understood as a test of our civilisation as a whole.

The three economic environmental functions are at stake. The supply of resources – directly to satisfy human needs, but also indirectly to allow the production of the goods and services our current wellbeing depends on –, the sink and assimilation of residuals from consumption and production activities, and the amenities function or the delivery of ecosystem services, clearly illustrate the multiple dimensions of the current ecological crisis. Our development model is demanding more natural resources than the environment can supply, thereby generating more residuals than the planet can absorb, and the equilibrium that has traditionally ruled interactions

---

[42] University of Coimbra, Faculty of Economics, Centre for Business and Economics Research.

[43] University of Coimbra, Faculty of Economics, Centre for Business and Economics Research.

https://doi.org/10.14195/978-989-26-2277-4_8

between man and the environment is being profoundly changed and at an unprecedent rate.

The urgency of explicitly considering the environment in our choices and the opportunity costs associated with the three economic functions of the environment, is as evident as the awareness that it is no longer possible to reduce this debate to the search for technical solutions capable of solving all problems. Humanity needs to find alternatives to deal with these increasingly serious challenges, which are at once systemic (changes, even if localised, tend to spread to the entire planet) and cumulative (small changes repeated over and over in numerous locations can lead to a global problem). These challenges must be projected beyond their material and quantitative aspects and take on the organizational and qualitative dimensions. Only by doing that will we be able to arrive at a better understanding of whether it isn't utopian to try to reconcile the objectives of social justice and equity, economic prosperity and preservation of the environment, and work, instead, to make it possible to gain competitiveness and efficiency while adopting more environmentally friendly production and consumption processes.

Jobs depend on the three economic functions of the environment in the same way economic activities integrate the world of work. Guillermo Montt argues that besides the worldwide network of jobs that depend directly on ecosystem services, environmental degradation further exacerbates risks that affect economic activity and is also a strong driver of growing inequality. Therefore, and considering that the current ecological crisis will continue to be a feature of our future, environmental degradation is also a major concern for the world of work, and a complex one.

The critical question addressed by Guillermo Montt is how can economic growth and environmental sustainability be made compatible with better, decent work. However, considering that we may have no option, that is to say, that environmental sustainability is compulsory, the way forward consists in envisaging what these environmentally sustainable, decent-work promoting economies will look like.

Taking as an example what a transition in the energy sector would entail for the world of work, the results presented involve, as might be expected, jobs created and jobs destroyed. Some parts of the world are likely to gain while others are projected to lose. But, overall, the net impacts are expected to be positive, both for the environment and for the world of work.

Given that a transition in the energy sector must combine structural changes at the supply and demand levels, a shift away from fossil fuels towards renewable energy sources, as well as improvements in energy efficiency, either in final consumption or production activities, will typically concentrate job losses in sectors like petroleum refining, crude petroleum extraction, production of electricity by coal and the mining of coal. On the other hand, jobs created will be mainly in the services sector, such as repair and rental services.

Finally, as always happens when dealing with a problem in which there are gains and losses, for different stakeholders and at different moments in time, it is essential to be aware that the net positive results will not be spontaneous and that it will be necessary to mobilise all those involved in the change. Above all, environmental degradation and unemployment are not necessarily inevitable. They result from policies that do not consider all the trade-offs involved and are the consequence of biased incentives that favour environmental degradation and encourage the use of virgin resources and exponential consumption.

Throughout human history, many civilisations have managed to reverse a trajectory of decline, including environmental degradation, thanks to cultural, political, social, economic and technological structural changes. Others, on the other hand, collapsed, particularly when the dominant class did not understand the nature of the degradation with which it was faced or when the technological and institutional capacity to innovate was not sufficient to adequately react. The future of work also depends on our foresight and ability to make the right political and individual choices. Guillermo Montt has made it clear that it is not possible to continue to resist and not change. We are aware of the challenges and we still have the freedom to choose our paths.

Each of us is simultaneously a consumer, a worker and a producer. As consumers, it is within our control to choose the products we want to consume, according to their environmental performance and appropriate modes of production (or to boycott those that show persistent negligence in respect of any of these dimensions). Simple ideas, followed by everyone, will have more effect than technological devices restricted to just a small number of users. More importantly, it is as consumers that we can modify our consumption patterns, for instance by favouring less resource-intensive goods directly extracted from the environment, or choosing use-as-a-service alternatives to the detriment of traditional, ownership-based use options. As voters, we have the opportunity to support political movements that advocate programs capable of promoting strategies that enable synergies between the environment and employment. As workers, our role is decisive: we can implement, namely by example, responsible attitudes towards the values of the environment and better conditions for the development of productive activities. Finally, as producers it is critical to pay continuous attention to the opportunity costs of using environmental resources, correct mistakes, share lessons and be receptive to opportunities for innovation and introduction of new, more environmentally friendly, production methods.

III.

INEQUALITIES, WORK AND GENDER GAPS

CHAPTER 5:
REDUCING INEQUALITY IN THE LABOUR MARKET[44]

Patrick Belser[45] and Khalid Maman Waziri[46]

Introduction

In a majority of countries around the world, and particularly in rich countries, income inequality has risen steeply since the 1980s, with adverse social and economic consequences.[47] In OECD countries, the average incomes of the top 10% recently reached almost ten times those of the bottom 10%, up from a ratio of 7 to 1 in the 1980s.[48] The Gini measure of income inequality for industrialised

---

[44] Part of this paper draws upon the International Labour Conference background paper: ILO, Inequalities and the world of work, ILC.109/IV (2021). This paper was received in May 2021 and is also a result of the participation of the first author in the webinar "Inequalities at work" (3rd edition of "Cátedra OIT/ILO Chair"), held at the University of Coimbra, Faculty of Economics (FEUC), on November 11, 2020.

[45] Patrick Belser is a Senior Economist, Wage Specialist, at the International Labour Organization (ILO) in Geneva.

[46] Khalid Maman Waziri is an Economist, Labour Economics specialist, at the ILO in Geneva. The views expressed in this article are those of the authors and do not necessarily reflect the views of the ILO. We thank Estefania Mujica Prado for excellent research assistance with income inequality data.

[47] See Salvatore Morelli et al., "Post-1970 trends in within-country inequality and poverty: Rich and middle-income countries", *Handbook of Income Distribution 2*, (2015), 593–696.

[48] OECD, *Understanding the socio-economic divide in Europe*, 2017.

https://doi.org/10.14195/978-989-26-2277-4_9

countries increased, on average, by 3 percentage points (from 30 to 33) between 1988 and 2008.[49] Globally, from 1990 to 2015, a majority of 77 out of 149 countries with available data experienced an increase in the Gini coefficient of inequality. In other countries, although income inequality stagnated or decreased, as in some countries in Latin America in the 1990s and early 2000s, inequality remains high and continues to divide societies.

In the shadows of the growing income inequality lie many different types of inequalities between men and women, young and old, migrants and nationals, inhabitants of mega-cities and semi-urban or rural areas, or between different racial and ethnic groups. These inequalities contribute to slicing up countries and stir resentments. In some countries, growing inequality lies at the root of social unrest, growing discontent among middle classes, and an unravelling social contract.[50] In more extreme cases, persistent inequalities and discrimination against specific groups can be a source of violent conflict.[51] Frequently, different layers of inequality intersect and accumulate, placing some groups of people – indigenous women in rural areas, for example – at the bottom of the pyramid and in a particularly vulnerable position.

The COVID-19 pandemic has highlighted and in many ways further deepened those growing inequalities.[52] People already disadvantaged before the pandemic have been exposed more severely than others, from catching the virus to dealing with the economic consequences of the pandemic. While some groups of people have been able to reduce their exposure to the risk of contagion by working from

---

[49] World Bank, *Taking on inequality*.

[50] OECD, *Under pressure*, 27–28.

[51] Frances Stewart (ed.) (2008), *Horizontal inequalities and conflict: Understanding group violence in multiethnic societies*. Palgrave: Macmillan UK.

[52] COVID-19: Protecting workers in the workplace: COVID-19 cruelly highlights inequalities and threatens to deepen them (ilo.org)

home or to deal with the consequences of the virus by going on sick leave, accessing health services and continuing to receive a salary, for others – particularly those at the bottom of the income chain – the scenario has been no less than catastrophic. Many were not covered by health insurance and may not even have had access to health services. Even if their health recovered, the absence of income replacement benefits meant that they have become poor.

This paper argues that reducing inequality has become an urgent priority, that it must be part of a human-centred recovery from the crisis, and that one key place to act is the labour market. There was already an emerging consensus before the pandemic that high levels of inequality can have major adverse human, social, economic and political consequences. This concern has been further heightened by the catastrophic impact of the pandemic. The central message of this paper is that labour markets in general – and the distribution of income from work in particular – are essential areas of action for reducing inequalities. While more fiscal redistribution through taxes and transfers is imperative to reduce inequalities, as advocated by the IMF and many others, there are limits to what redistribution alone can achieve – particularly in developing countries where fiscal space is limited and when the growth of inequality originates in the labour market. Decent work for all and a fair distribution of income from work are essential components of any strategy to reduce inequality.

I: Some facts and figures about income inequality

Data on income inequality can sometimes be difficult to absorb and interpret. Most data sources provide information on either inequality in market income (pre-tax and pre-transfer) and/or in disposable income (post-tax, post-transfer). The most widely used indicator of inequality, the Gini coefficient, takes a value which ranges from zero when there is perfect equality (everybody has the same income) to 1 when there is total inequality (all the income only goes to one person). Using the data from the Standardized World Income Inequality Database (SWIID), a dataset which homogenises observations from different sources[53], Figure 1 illustrates the variability of income inequality across countries, displaying the most recently available Gini value (2016 or 2015 in most of the cases). We can observe that Gini coefficients range from less than 25 in Slovakia, Belarus or Iceland to values around 60 in Botswana, Eswatini, South Africa and Namibia – the most unequal countries in the world according to this data. Among high-income countries, inequality is relatively low in Denmark, Sweden or the Netherlands, and relatively high in the United States. In many low- and middle--income countries, including China, Mexico, Brazil or India, inequality is higher than in the United States. It has been observed previously that Sub-Saharan Africa and Latin America & the Caribbean are the two regions with the highest inequality.[54]

---

[53] See Solt, Frederick (2020), "Measuring Income Inequality Across Countries and Over Time: The Standardized World Income Inequality Database." *Social Science Quarterly*. SWIID Version 9.1, May 2021.

[54] See World Bank, *Taking on inequality*.

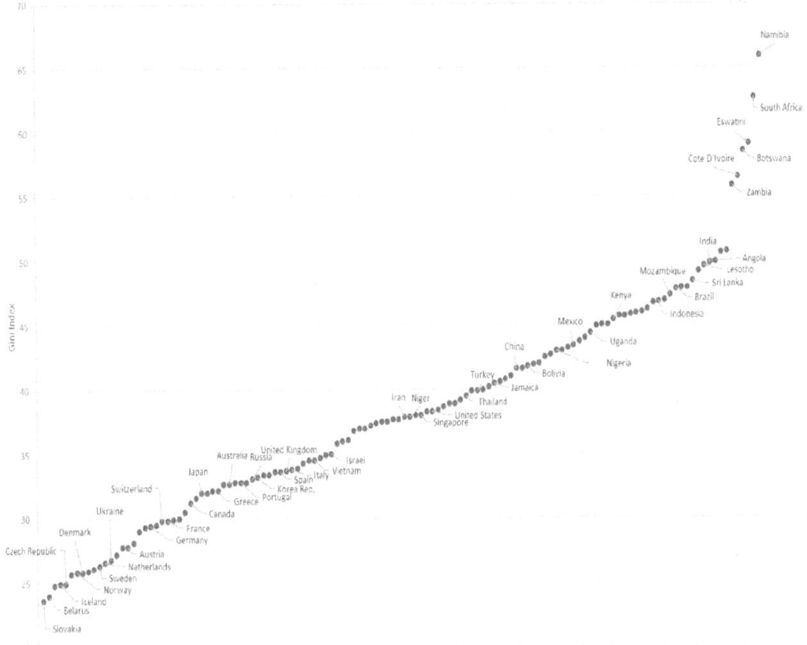

Source: Standardized World Income Inequality Database, May 2021.
Note: Disposable income from 2016 or 2015 are used for the Gini coefficient estimates.

While the Gini coefficient allows for comparisons across countries (or within countries over time), one shortcoming of this measure of inequality is that it has no intuitive meaning. Another drawback is that a given Gini value can result from very different underlying distributions. Hence, in recent years, interest has shifted to the more appealing measure of "income shares": the income share of the richest 1%, 10% or 50% of the population in proportion to the total incomes earned by all households in a country. Figure 2 below shows the share of total income obtained by the top 10%, according to the World Inequality Lab database (2019). According to these estimates, in South Africa – one of the most unequal countries in the world (as we have already observed with the Gini value) – more than 65% of total income is obtained by the richest 10%. In India, Mexico and Brazil, which are also very unequal countries, the top 10% obtain between 57 and 59% of total incomes. In the United States, the income share of the top 10% reaches approximately 45%, which implies more inequality than in China, where this share is around 42%, and considerably more inequality than in Western Europe, where this share ranges typically between 29 and 38%. It is noteworthy that in this database, Gulf countries – for which Gini estimates are usually missing – display extremely high levels of inequality.

Figure 2: The income shares of the top 10% in selected countries

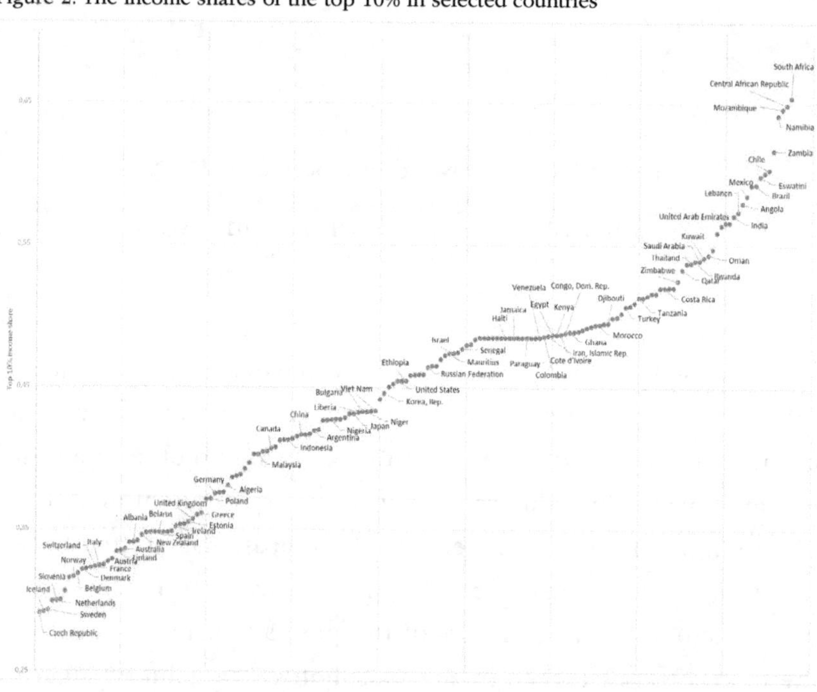

Source: World Inequality Database, 2019 top 10%
share of pre-tax national income.

Another difficulty with income inequality data is often related to inconsistent rankings of levels of inequality. Figure 3 compares rankings derived from World Bank and World Inequality Database (WID) estimates of income shares held by the richest 10%. As can be seen, there is some consensus on which countries have the highest and the lowest levels of inequality. However, at the middle of the distribution, the rankings are less consistent. This is particularly the case with the United Arab Emirates. Such disparities might be explained by the source of the data used to construct the inequality indicators. While the World Bank uses income or consumption data from household surveys, the WID indicator uses pre-tax income distribution. In addition, the WID overcomes the income data limitations of national household surveys by combining these data with several other data sources, including national accounts, survey data, fiscal data, and wealth rankings.

Furthermore, Figure 4 shows that the same consensus prevails when the Gini is used to observe in which countries inequality is highest or lowest. However, Figure 5 and particularly Figure 6, where only OECD countries are presented, show a greater consistency, even at the middle of the distribution, in the rankings of inequality levels. This suggests that data collected from more developed countries, which are generally characterised by better availability and quality of statistical data, manage to capture better, and with more precision, the differences in inequality levels across countries – pointing towards the difficulties of estimating inequality with precision in developing countries. In Figure 6, the rankings are even more consistent because both indicators use similar income distributions.

Figure 3: Coherence of the ranking for the income share held by highest 10% estimates (2014 or 2015)

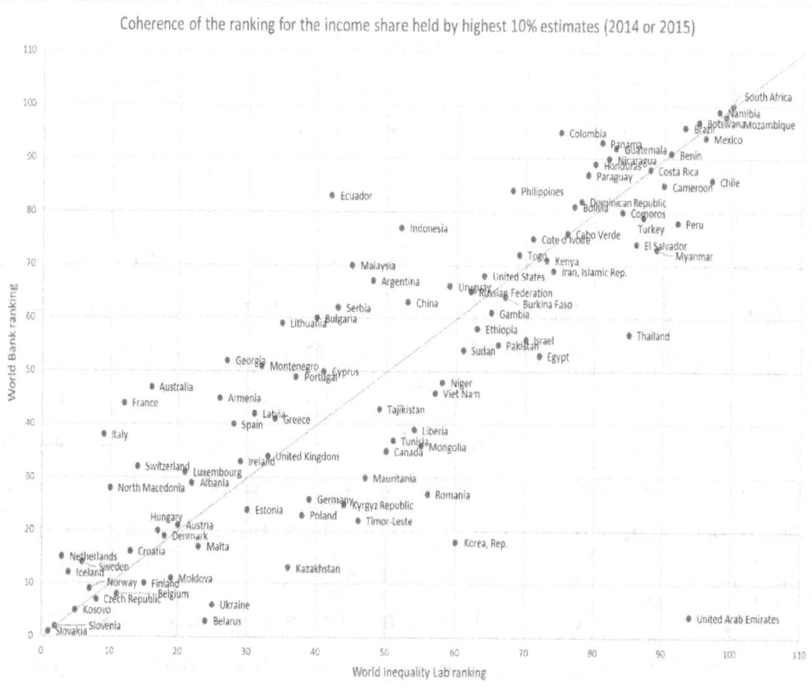

Notes: World Bank uses income or consumption data from primary household surveys, while World Inequality Lab uses pre-tax income obtained from different sources. For the following 20 countries (out of a total of 100), 2014 estimates are used: Argentina, Australia, Burkina Faso, Cameroon, Comoros, Guatemala, Israel, Korea Republic, Liberia, Mauritania, Mexico, Mongolia, Mozambique, Nicaragua, Niger, South Africa, Sudan, East Timor, United Arab Emirates, Vietnam.

Figure 4: Coherence of the ranking for the Gini coefficient, World Bank and SWIID, 2015

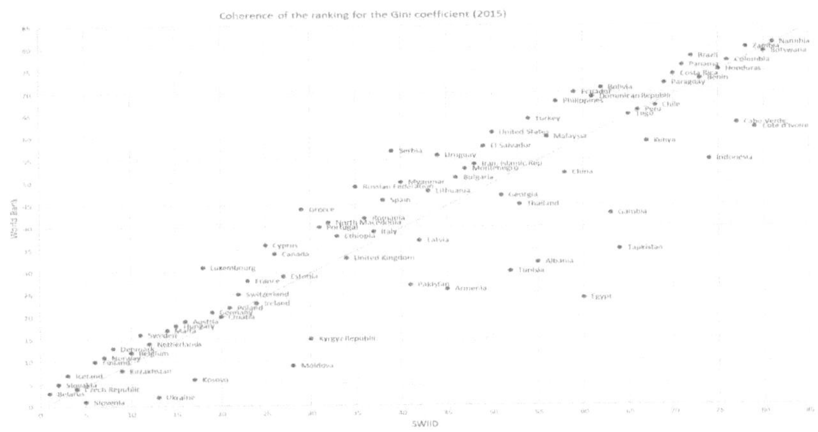

Notes: World Bank uses income or consumption data from primary household surveys, while SWIID uses disposable income obtained from different sources which are standardised.

Figure 5: Coherence of the ranking for the Gini coefficient, World Bank and OECD, 2016

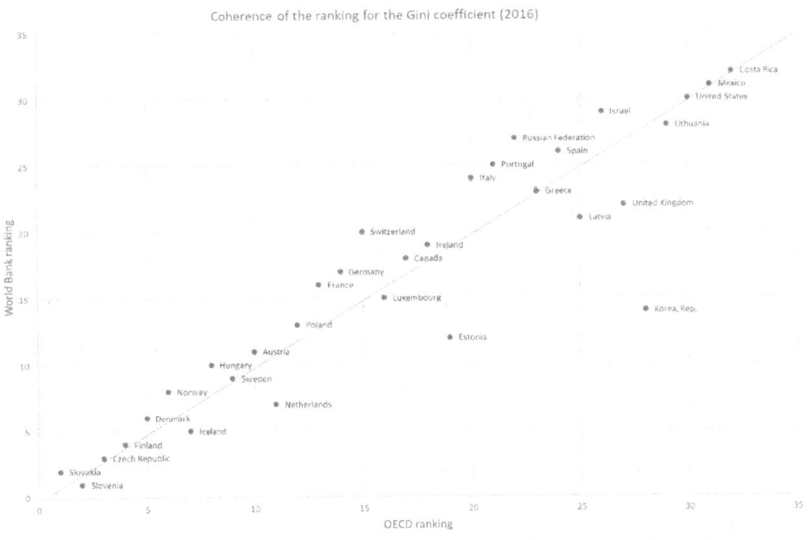

Notes: World Bank uses income or consumption data from primary household surveys, while OECD uses disposable income distributions.

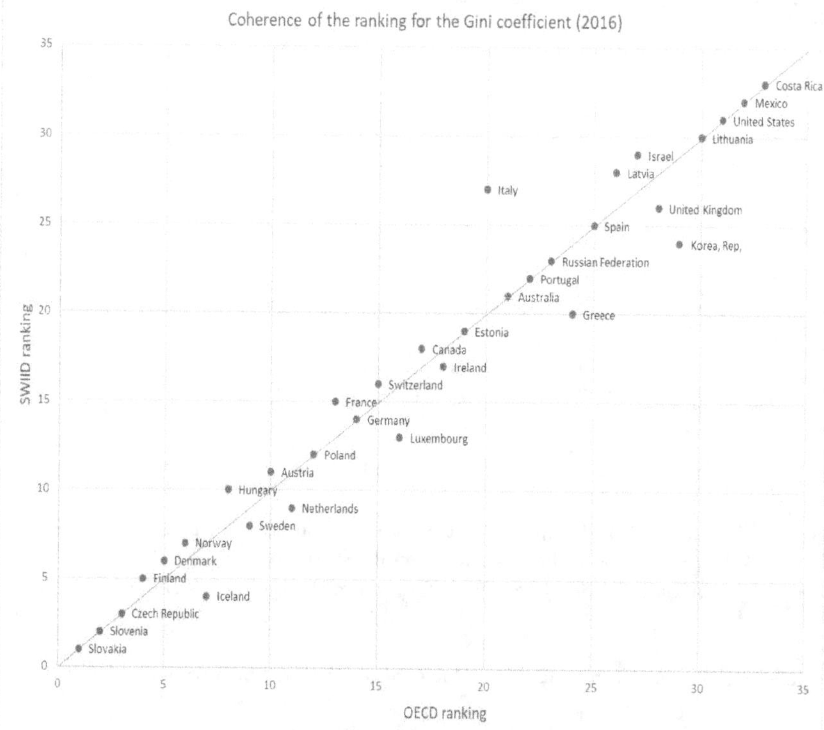

Notes: SWIID uses disposable income obtained from different sources which are standardised, while OECD uses disposable income distributions

Reducing inequality within countries requires an understanding of who the low-income people are. In South Africa, for example, inequality between Black and Whites remains a defining feature of overall income inequality. The average income of a Black African person represents only just 15% of the average income of a White person, which is to say that White people earn about 6.5 times more income than Black Africans. Inequality is also geographic, as incomes in rural areas are about 4 times less than in urban areas.[55]

---

[55] Stat SA, Inequality trends in South Africa Report, 2020 Report-03-10-192017.pdf (statssa.gov.za).

In Brazil, the rate of poverty among Afro-descendants, who represent more than half of the total population, is twice as high as for non Afro-descendants.[56] In India, Scheduled Tribes and Scheduled Castes have persistently worse outcomes across health, education, and monetary indicators.[57] In the United States, the median black household income was 61% of median white household income in 2018.[58] Within Gulf countries, the high levels of inequality are in large part a reflection of the high number – and much lower incomes – of migrant workers. Even if much inequality also exists within groups, reducing these "horizontal" inequalities between groups is an indispensable component of any strategy to reduce inequality.

II. The possible consequences of high inequality, and the resolve to reduce inequality

In recent years, a growing number of studies have documented the negative effects of high inequality. As emphasized in the World Inequality Report, rising inequality can lead to all sorts of human, political, economic and social catastrophes.[59] Indeed, in the past, inequality has sometimes been seen as a natural side-product of economic development and a necessary condition for a country to increase its rate of investment and economic growth. Recent research, including by the IMF and the OECD, has tended to emphasize the adverse effects of high inequality.

First, it has been observed that high levels of inequality erode social cohesion and increase the risk of social unrest. Indeed, equi-

---

[56] 25% versus 11%. See COVID-19 Reports: People of African descent and COVID-19: unveiling structural inequalities in Latin America (cepal.org).

[57] WIDER Policy Brief 2018/6 – Inequality in India on the rise (unu.edu).

[58] 6 facts about economic inequality in the U.S. | Pew Research Center.

[59] *World inequality report* 2018. P.4).

table societies with strong and prosperous middle classes contribute to more cohesive societies, have lower crime rates, enjoy higher levels of trust and life satisfaction, and have greater political stability.[60] By contrast, rising income inequality tends to be associated with higher criminality and lower social capital formation.[61] High inequality can become politically unsustainable, as it undermines public trust in policies and institutions and leads to popular discontent.[62] The World Bank points out that "in more cohesive societies, threats arising from extremism, political turmoil, and institutional fragility are less likely".[63]

Secondly, high or rising income inequality also hurts social mobility. Policy debates sometimes focus on the importance of ensuring equality of opportunity for all individuals, rather than on income inequality per se.[64] In practice, however, equality of opportunity and equality of incomes are correlated. In other words, countries with greater income inequality also tend to be those with reduced intergenerational social mobility – where it is more difficult for individuals to move to an earnings class different to the one into which they were born.[65] This relationship also holds in different geographical areas within countries. In an interesting study, Chetty et al. (2014) show that areas in the United States with high social

---

[60] OECD 2019 *Under pressure: The squeezed middle class.*

[61] D'Hombres, Weber and Leandro, 2012.

[62] OECD, 2019 *Under pressure: The squeezed middle class*; OECD, *Divided we stand.*

[63] World Bank, *Taking on inequality*, p.3.

[64] Equal opportunity refers to a situation in which all people would be "equally enabled to make the best of such powers as they possess" (definition by Richard Tawney, quoted in Anthony B. Atkinson, *Inequality: What can be done?* (Harvard University Press, 2015, 9), or alternatively as "a situation in which circumstances that are beyond personal control (such as family background or sex) do not play a role in determining inequality of outcome" (John Roemer, as quoted in Atkinson, *Inequality: What can be done?*).

[65] Miles Corak, "Income inequality, equality of opportunity, and intergenerational mobility", *Journal of Economic Perspectives* 27, No. 3 (2013), 79–102.

mobility are places which have, among several things, less income inequality.[66]

Thirdly, high inequality can have adverse macroeconomic effects. Recent IMF research has demonstrated that high levels of inequality are harmful for the pace and sustainability of economic growth[67], and hence that lower inequality is correlated with faster and more robust growth. Similarly, OECD research has shown that greater social and economic inclusion is strongly associated with longer and stronger periods of sustained economic growth[68]. Part of the reason for the slower economic growth in high-inequality countries has to do with inequality's adverse effect on a country's investment in skills and education. In many countries, growing inequality also has a negative impact on aggregate demand, as it limits the consumption demand of the lower and middle classes and increases the savings of the rich.[69]

Finally, last but not least, when economic growth is combined with growing inequality, the link between growth and poverty reduction is weakened. In developing countries, persistent or growing inequalities mean that in spite of economic growth many million low-income households remain unable to adequately cover the cost of their basic needs. In spite of important progress in recent decades, there were – even before the COVID-19 crisis – more than 750 million people, representing more than 10% of the global population, living below the very modest international poverty line of US$1.90 per day.[70] Hence the SDG goal of eliminating extreme poverty by 2030 might not be achieved without reductions of inequalities wi-

---

[66] Chetty, et al. (2014), Where is the land of opportunity? The geography of intergenerational mobility in the United States. NBER Working paper No. 19843.

[67] Ostry, Berg and Tsangarides, 2014.

[68] OECD, 2014a.

[69] See ILO, *Global Wage Report 2012/13*, Wages and equitable growth.

[70] World Bank *Taking on inequality*, p.3.

thin countries, particularly countries with large concentrations of poor people.[71]

For all these and maybe other reasons, growing inequality has emerged as a major concern in recent years – a concern which the coronavirus disease (COVID-19) pandemic has further heightened. Central to the global efforts to reduce inequality is the United Nations (UN) 2030 Agenda for Sustainable Development (2030 Agenda), which pledges that "no one will be left behind". Sustainable Development Goal (SDG) Number 10 focuses specifically on the objective of reducing inequality within and among countries, including through "fiscal, wage and social protection" policies. In addition, the objective of reducing inequalities cuts across all of the SDGs and is also reflected in their respective targets, which call for disaggregation by gender, age and rural-urban location, all of which are important dimensions of inequality.[72]

While reducing inequality in many of its different manifestations and promoting the principle of equality of opportunity and treatment have always been inherent in the mandate and instruments of the International Labour Organization (ILO), other multilateral institutions have also recently strengthened their work on inequality. The World Bank has expanded its mandate beyond the elimination of extreme poverty and promotes "shared prosperity", seeking to foster the income growth of the poorest 40% of the population.[73] The International Monetary Fund (IMF) has documented the adverse impact of high levels of inequality on economic growth in a series of studies and has included inequality issues in its country work.[74] The Organization for Economic Co-operation and Development

---

[71] World Bank *Taking on inequality*.

[72] United Nations General Assembly, Transforming our world: The 2030 agenda for sustainable development, A/RES/70/1, 21 October 2015.

[73] World Bank website, www.worldbank.org.

[74] IMF, "The IMF and income inequality", n.d.

(OECD) has published a series of flagship reports on inequality, launched a New Approaches to Economic Challenges initiative and an Inclusive Growth initiative, and created the Centre for Opportunity and Equality as a platform for policy-oriented research on inequalities.[75] As a final example, the Human Development Report 2019 of the United Nations Development Programme (UNDP) was devoted to inequalities.[76]

III. What can be done? The important role of labour markets

When it comes to reducing income inequality, the most frequent policy recommendations probably lie in the field of education and fiscal redistribution. Education is central to empowering disadvantaged groups and raising their earnings potential. For many people, the experience of inequality starts at birth – when they are disadvantaged because of their gender, the colour of their skin, or because they never received a birth certificate. These factors can translate into various other forms of inequality later in life, for example unequal opportunity in accessing good quality education or health care. Fiscal redistribution through taxes and transfers is central too. Indeed, a country's system of tax and transfers can redistribute income so that households can enjoy greater levels of equality in respect of disposable income. The incidence of redistribution through tax and transfers on income inequality depends on many factors, including the amount of taxes levied and distributed and the progressivity of taxation and transfers. In other words, the extent to which high-income earners pay a bigger share of their

---

[75] OECD, "Inequality", n.d.

[76] UNDP, *Human development report 2019: Beyond income, beyond averages, beyond today – Inequalities in human development in the 21st century*, 2019.

income in taxes than low-income earners and the extent to which, proportionally, transfers benefit low-income families more than high-income families.[77]

It is however also essential to recognise the limits in dealing with growing inequality only through fiscal redistribution, especially since in recent years much of the growth in income inequality originated in more unequal market incomes (before taxes and transfers). Another reality is that in recent years the tax systems of many countries have become less progressive,[78] through the introduction of fewer tax brackets, the reduction of top marginal tax rates or the adoption of flat tax schemes.[79] Furthermore, in developing countries, there is relatively limited scope for redistribution through taxes and transfers because of limited fiscal resources, a problem compounded by high informality. A more comprehensive approach is thus needed, which includes action to make labour markets and incomes from work more equitable.

Let us start with the importance of employment. According to the OECD, an increase of 1 percentage point in the share of employment reduces income inequality (measured by the Gini coefficient) by 0.65 percentage points.[80] Unfortunately, in 2019, prior to the outbreak of the COVID-19 pandemic, there were already an estimated 188 million people in unemployment around the world, equivalent to an unemployment rate of 5% (6% for women and 5% for men).

---

[77] See: Keeley Brian (2015), "How Does Income Inequality Affect Our Lives", *Income inequality: The gap between rich and poor,* Chapter 4, OECD Insights. Paris: OECD Publishing.

[78] A progressive tax system requires those with higher incomes (or greater wealth) to contribute a larger share of their income (or wealth) to general government revenues. Malte Luebker (2015), "Redistribution Policies", *Labour markets, institutions and inequality: Building just societies in the 21st century,* ed. Janine Berg (Edward Elgar/ILO).

[79] Salvador Barrios et al. (2019), "Progressive tax reforms in flat tax countries", Euromod Working Paper Series EM 2/19.

[80] OECD (2011), *Divided we stand: Why inequality keeps rising.*

The COVID-19 crisis has magnified the problem. Moreover, the rate of unemployment was almost three times higher among young people.[81] When individuals or certain groups are more likely to be unemployed, their income prospects are compromised.

While unemployment is a widely used indicator, this measure of labour "underutilisation" is less useful in countries where informality or inactivity, rather than unemployment, characterise people's responses to insufficient opportunities for formal economy work. A more comprehensive measure of labour underutilisation is thus used by the ILO, which, in addition to unemployed individuals, takes into account people in work who would like to work more paid hours ("time-related underemployment") and people out of employment who would like to work but who are not actively searching for a job or are not available for work ("the potential labour force"). In 2019, this composite measure accounted for 13.1% of the global workforce (or 473 million people), a figure that is considerably higher than the rate of unemployment (5%). It included 165 million people in time-related underemployment and an estimated 119 million people in the potential labour force, in addition to the 188 million people who were unemployed.[82] This measure captures an especially large share of the workforce in low-income countries (a rate of 20%, compared to an unemployment rate of 4%), signaling major obstacles to people's opportunities to access paid work.

Among those who work, inequality in the distribution of wages and labour incomes is among the most important determinants of inequality. In many high-income countries, growing wage inequality – with large gains at the top of the distribution and stagnating or declining relative wages of workers with lower levels of educa-

---

[81] ILO (2020), *World employment and social outlook: Trends 2020.*

[82] ILO (2020), *World employment and social outlook: Trends 2020.*

tion and skills at the bottom[83] – has been identified as the single most important factor driving higher income inequality in recent decades.[84] This is relatively unsurprising, since wages from paid employment are, in this category of countries, the largest source of household income, accounting for 70-80% on average.[85] In many countries, growing wage inequality took place alongside job polarisation, where the reduction in the number of middle-skilled and middle-paid jobs pushed many workers into low-skilled and low-paid jobs, or out of work entirely.[86] In some middle-income countries, a reduction of inequality in labour earnings has contributed to a fall in income inequality. In various Latin American countries, a reduction in wage inequality – as a result of sharp increases in wages at the bottom of the distribution, including through formalisation, as well as narrowing wage gaps between urban and rural regions and between ethnic minorities and the majority of the population – has been identified as one of the main drivers of reduced income inequality since the late 1990s.[87]

To protect workers against unduly low pay and to reduce wage inequality at the lower end of the distribution, many countries have, in recent years, adopted new minimum wages or strengthened existing ones. Germany and South Africa, both of which operated a limited number of sectoral minimum wages, adopted new national minimum wages in 2015 and 2019, respectively. In 2020, Qatar be-

---

[83] OECD, *Understanding the socio-economic divide in Europe.*

[84] OECD, "Time to act: Making inclusive growth happen", OECD Policy Brief, 2017; Luebker, "Redistribution policies".

[85] ILO, *Global wage report 2014/15: Wages and income inequality,* 2015, xvii; see also: Edward Webster, Imraan Valodia and David Francis (eds.) (2020), *Towards a Southern approach to inequality: Inequality studies in South Africa and the Global South.* London: Routledge.

[86] OECD, *OECD Employment outlook 2019: The future of work,* 2019, box 3.1.

[87] Julián Messina and Joana Silva (2016), *Wage inequality in Latin America*; Carlos Rodríguez-Castelán et al., "Understanding the dynamics of labor income inequality in Latin America", World Bank Policy Research Working Paper No. 7795.

came the first Gulf country to adopt a non-discriminatory minimum wage for nationals and foreign workers alike. In a step towards making minimum wages more inclusive, India extended the coverage of minimum wages from a list of so-called "scheduled" jobs to all wage workers in the country. Such measures have the potential to reduce wage and income inequalities, including gender pay gaps.[88] The extent to which they do so, however, depends on a number of factors, including whether the minimum wage has broad legal coverage, enjoys strong compliance by employers, or is fixed at an adequate level that takes into account the needs of workers and their families and economic factors.[89] Because non-compliance is a major problem facing the informal workforce, minimum wages are more effective at reducing inequalities when they are accompanied by measures to formalise the informal economy.[90]

Well-functioning collective bargaining mechanisms are also a powerful tool to ensure a fair share of the fruits of progress to wage earners and reduce inequalities. Collective bargaining can have a broad equality-inducing effect by promoting fair wage structures, as well as other attributes of inclusive labour markets, including equal treatment, employee engagement and skills development. Empirical evidence from developed countries shows that inequality tends to be lower in countries where a large number of workers are covered by collective agreements.[91] When multi-employer arrangements

---

[88] Dale Belman and Paul J. Wolfson, *What does the minimum wage do?* (W.E. Upjohn Institute for Employment Research, 2014); Arindrajit Dube, "Impacts of minimum wages: Review of the international evidence", Independent Report, United Kingdom Government Publication, 2019; Jill Rubery and Damian Grimshaw (2011), "Gender and the minimum wage", *Regulating for decent work: New directions in labour market regulation*, ed. Sangheon Lee and Deirdre McCann. London: Palgrave Macmillan, 226-254.

[89] The Centenary Declaration calls for the implementation of "an adequate minimum wage, statutory or negotiated".

[90] See ILO *Global wage report 2020-21.*

[91] OECD, *Negotiating our way up: Collective bargaining in a changing world of work,* 2019.

cover a whole sector or region, they tend to favour wage increases for workers at the low end of the income distribution. Some countries apply extension provisions, sometimes subject to "opt-out" clauses, to apply the terms of collective agreements beyond their signatories, thereby extending the impact on equality to a larger share of the workforce. Unfortunately, in many countries and most particularly low-income countries, collective bargaining covers relatively few workers, especially at the low end of the wage scale where informality is high.

There are however multiple challenges in reducing earnings inequalities through wage-setting institutions. In the following paragraph we highlight two of them: the high levels of informality in many developing countries, and the emergence of digital labour platforms.

The effectiveness of many means of reducing inequality depends on the formalisation of the economy. Minimum wage systems and collective bargaining are indeed not most effective to reducing inequality in the labour market in a context where the majority of workers are in the informal economy, and so are many other instruments. The recent unprecedented crisis of the COVID-19 should, in any case, serve as a wake-up call to accelerate progress in the transition to formality if we want to build more resilient and fairer societies. Indeed, the formalisation of the economy should enable those countries with a large informal economy, mainly the low-and middle-income countries, to have a larger tax base, which would allow them to implement more effective redistributive measures and achieve better coverage in terms of social protection, especially in times of crises.[92] Because of earnings differentials between the informal and formal economies, formalisation of the economy is also the surest path to reducing earnings inequality, and beyond

---

[92] IMF, "The Informal economy and inclusive growth".

that, an effective way to reducing poverty, which is particularly high among informal economy workers.[93]

Successful examples of reducing inequality through the formalisation of the economy are evident in many countries in Latin America, such as Argentina, Brazil, Mexico, Peru and Uruguay, which managed to considerably reduce income inequality since the late 1990s.[94] In these countries, the formalisation of the economy has relied on a combination of multifaceted policies, including tax benefits and simplifications, simplification of administrative procedures, policies to improve access to banking and financial services for small businesses and informal workers, awareness-raising of both employers and workers. In Brazil, for example, the Simples Federal regime, which simplified the tax and social security system, permitted the registration of 7 million people under the individual micro-entrepreneur regime, and about 5 million micro and small enterprises under the monotax regime, encompassing almost 11 million employees (about a quarter of all formal employees in Brazil).[95]

As new technologies develop, reducing inequality will also require policies to ensure better protections for the new types of jobs that have emerged. While digital labour platforms have per-

---

[93] There exist significant income disparities between the formal and the informal economy. See ILO (2021), *Inequalities and the world of work*, ILC.109/IV; Informal economy workers are twice more likely to be poor – see ILO (2018), *Women and men in the informal economy: A Statistical picture*, third edition, 13.

[94] Julián Messina and Joana Silva, *Wage inequality in Latin America*, 58. See also: Francisco H.G. Ferreira, Sergio P. Firpo and Julián Messina, "Ageing poorly? Accounting for the decline in earnings inequality in Brazil, 1995–2012", World Bank Policy Research Working Paper No. 8018, 2017, who find that the reduction of the wage gap between formal and informal work from 1995 to 2012 in Brazil contributed to a reduction of 1.7 points out of the 9-point reduction in the Gini measure of income inequality. A significant impact in Uruguay is also reported by Verónica Amarante, Rodrigo Arim and Mijail Yapor (2016), "Decomposing inequality changes in Uruguay: The Role of formalization in the labor market", *IZA Journal of Labor & Development* 5, No. 1, 13.

[95] ILO (2019), *Simples national: Monotax regime for own-account workers, micro and small entrepreneurs – Experiences from Brazil.*

mitted the rise of many new work and income opportunities for many people, this rise has been accompanied by many challenges that threaten to accelerate the growth of inequality. Indeed, many workers on digital platforms have found themselves in a similar situation to workers in the informal economy, suffering from a "misclassification issue" that denies them access to employee rights, notably labour and social protections.[96] This is particularly because their working conditions are regulated unilaterally by the digital platforms' terms of service agreements. Being outside the scope of labour regulations, these new types of workers could not claim a minimum wage, nor exercise their right to freedom of association and collective bargaining, especially for self-employed digital platform workers. In addition, with the emergence of these new types of jobs, additional earnings disparities have emerged, especially between developing and developed countries, a gap that reaches 60% on freelance platforms, even after controlling for basic characteristics and types of tasks performed. Reducing inequality will therefore also require regulations to prevent and contain the emergence of such new inequalities. In some countries, such as in the United Kingdom – where Uber drivers have recently obtained the right to unionise –, digital platform workers are beginning to organise to demand more rights. However, these workers often lack bargaining power. Consequently, new initiatives and ideas are needed to ensure better labour and social protections for these new types of workers.

Conclusion

This paper has shown how inequalities have increased in recent years and particularly affect certain groups of people who are di-

---

[96] ILO (2021), *World employment and social outlook 2021: The Role of digital labour platforms in transforming the world of work.*

sadvantaged from birth, especially because of their gender, or skin color, or origin, etc., while other groups benefited more from the fruits of progress in recent years. This threatens social peace as well as many economic and poverty reduction gains. This paper has shown that redistribution and transfer policies do have merit in reducing inequality, but that these alone will not be able to effectively contain the increase in inequality, particularly in countries characterised by a large informal economy. This is especially relevant since the consequences of the unprecedented COVID-19 crisis has exacerbated the hardships to which many groups of people were already exposed, including women, youth, workers in the informal economy, and all those other workers whose contracts or form of employment offer little or no employment and social protections.

Effectively reducing inequality will therefore require urgent actions through the labour market, which creates and shapes many inequalities of opportunity, outcome and treatment, most of which are perpetuated over generations. Indeed, when individuals do not have access to jobs, or when the jobs to which they have access do not allow them to satisfy their needs and those of their families, many inequalities will appear, notably in access to health and education. This will particularly hamper the formation of their children's human capital, thus condemning several generations of the same group of individuals to be at a disadvantage in the labour markets and in societies. This is precisely why it will be necessary to have adequate wage policies that can protect low-paid workers so that they can have incomes that allow them to provide a decent standard of living for their families. Minimum wage systems and collective bargaining are examples of wage policies that have proven to be effective in reducing inequality by protecting workers from unduly low wages. However, as we have seen, such an effectiveness is only possible in the context of a large formal economy. Thus, in conjunction with wage policies, it will be necessary to accelerate the transition to a formal economy, which is a fundamental condition for effectively reducing inequality, particularly in developing countries.

Furthermore, the recent COVID-19 crisis has shown that the low resilience of our countries to shocks is another important source of rising inequalities. When crises strike, it is the most disadvantaged who are the most affected, as they are generally an adjustment variable in the labour market – therefore the first to lose their employment –, they lack social protection, and most often they lack savings to withstand the crisis. After the crisis, these disadvantaged groups of individuals will find themselves in an even more difficult or precarious situation than the initial one, which means a further increase in inequalities. This explains how the COVID-19 crisis could exacerbate inequalities. For instance, the World Bank estimates that the crisis could increase the number of people in extreme poverty in the world for the first time since 1998, by 88-115 million people.[97] The kind of shocks we experienced with COVID-19 could resurface in the years to come, notably because of the effects of climate change, technological change disruptions, other pandemics, or conflicts in certain areas. To prevent these shocks from increasing the already existing and high inequalities, as was the case with COVID-19, it is necessary to act now to create stronger, more equitable and more resilient labour markets.

---

[97] World Bank (2020), *Poverty and shared prosperity 2020: Reversals of fortune.*

COMMENT:

LABOUR MARKET AND INEQUALITIES

Luís Moura Ramos[98] and Margarida Antunes[99]

1. Main ideas of Belser and Waziri

The central message of the chapter is very clear: "labour markets in general – and the distribution of income from work in particular – are essential areas of action for reducing inequalities." This idea appears as a response to growing income inequality. This, in turn, is seen as the major concern of recent years, and reducing it is considered by the authors to be an urgent priority.

Belser and Waziri begin by analysing income inequality across the world based on Gini coefficients and the income shares of the top 10% calculated from different statistical sources, and by discussing the social and economic negative effects of income inequality known in the recent literature.

The third section is central to the whole chapter. The authors briefly review the most frequent recommendations and economic policies addressing this inequality, based on primary and secondary distribution of income. For the authors, policy action must focus on

---

[98] University of Coimbra, Faculty of Economics, Centre for Business and Economics Research.

[99] University of Coimbra, Faculty of Economics, Centre for Business and Economics Research.

https://doi.org/10.14195/978-989-26-2277-4_10

the primary distribution of income and they present two reasons. One is the current limitations of tax policies due to the diminished progressivity of tax systems and the low level of public tax receipts in developing countries resulting from high economic informality. The other is the high level of market income inequality which needs to be reverted. Accordingly, the authors argue for policies that reduce inequality in the labour market, which is the principal object of analysis.

Belser and Waziri propose policies targeting non-employed people as well as the distribution of wages and other labour incomes, with a primary focus on wage-setting institutions. Related to the former, they only propose the use of the labour underutilisation rate instead of the unemployment rate in policy design. It is a more comprehensive indicator of the social fragilities of the labour market, since it includes halos of unemployment such as time-related underemployed, discouraged workers and also other inactive persons who for example are looking for work but are not currently available for work. To reduce wage inequality, the authors call attention to four aspects. First, the importance of the minimum wage, which should be improved in the countries where it is already in place and created in those in which it is not, in which case it must be accompanied by a reduction in informality. Both policies must be pursued in the context of social consultation. Second, well-functioning mechanisms of collective bargaining, which promote equal treatment of workers – favouring low paid workers and thereby reducing wage inequality – and facilitate the development of skills. Third, the decline in informality in developing countries, which, given the positive differential between the wage levels in the formal and informal economy, leads to a rise in wages and extends the number of workers covered by the two previous mechanisms. This policy allows the creation or improvement of social protection for all workers in the informal economy, although this effect can be also considered a result of secondary distribution of income. Fourth, the improvement of labour and social protections for jobs resulting from new digital technologies, such as digital platforms, for which a legal status for workers has not yet been created, a fact that prevents these workers from benefiting from the first two mechanisms.

2. Some reflections

Belser and Waziri's chapter has the merit of highlighting the importance of primary distribution of income in the reduction of income inequality. Redistribution policies occur only after the generation of income, and in this sense are considered *ex-post* policies or "post-production policies", as Rodrik and Stantcheva (2021, p.1) call them. In contrast, primary distribution occurs at the stage of production and so results from decisions on investment, employment, wage setting and profit creation. In other words, it occurs at the root of income creation.

With the primary distribution of income having these characteristics, the four aspects analysed by Belser and Waziri are appropriate solutions to reduce labour market inequality. However, there are other aspects inherent in the current functioning of the labour market that should be included in the analysis.

The labour income inequality resulting from the labour income levels of higher income groups is a fundamental element of income inequality since the 1980's (International Labour Organization [ILO], 2008; Atkinson et al. 2011; Baker et al., 2019). In the USA, the CEO-to-typical-worker pay ratio rose from 188-to-1 in 2009, a year in which it declined due to the financial crisis, to 312-to-1 in 2017 (Mishel & Schieder, 2018). The highest wages are one of the explanations put forward by Berman and Milanovic (2020) for homoploutia, a situation in which the same people are both capital-income rich and labour-income rich. This phenomenon has increased in the USA and, according to Berman and Milanovic, is a contributory factor to the rise in income inequality.

Still on labour income, Belser and Waziri should have analysed the wage inequality resulting from labour contracts that are to the detriment of workers with non-standard employment such as temporary jobs, part-time jobs and disguised employment. They mention the case of digital labour platforms and workers in the informal economy, but other workers are also subject to contractual and wage insecurity. As a share of total employment this has increased in all regions of the world (ILO, 2016), which has implications for wage inequality. In the case of temporary work, taking into account differences in the age, education, occupation and sector of activity, for similar workers and occupations there is a wage gap of up to 30% compared to workers on open-ended contracts (ILO, 2016, 2021). In the European Union-27, since 2010, the incidence of "in-work at-risk-of-poverty jobs in temporary employment has been almost three times that of permanent employment, while in for part-time employment it is approximately twice that of full-time employment. In addition, lower wages and insecure jobs mean that workers do not benefit or benefit less from the secondary distribution of income, because their social security payments or their jobs tenure limit the access to this right.

Belser and Waziri do not consider external economic mechanisms of the labour market that also determine the labour income inequality and that are present at the production stage. This market cannot be analysed as if it were disconnected from the formation of other incomes, such as capital income, and hence from decisions on investment and employment. Economic policy also influences wage setting and employment through mechanisms other than the minimum wage and collective bargaining legislation.

The increase in labour income inequality has been accompanied by a decline in labour income as a share of national incomes in both developed countries and developing countries (ILO, 2008; International Monetary Fund [IMF], 2017). This trend is already related to the distribution of income between labour and capital, and an understanding of it makes apparent other important aspects linked to external mechanisms of the labour market. Usually, the main reasons given are technological change and capital and trade globalisation, which have reduced the low-and middle-skills labour content of production processes. This has lowered the bargaining power of workers and limited the wage increases in developed countries (European Commission, 2007; IMF, 2007). In developing countries, the host countries of the low-tech techniques, there may also be an upgrading of production processes to the detriment of unskilled labour. The Global Value Chains (GVCs) are representatives of these aspects and are therefore better analysed in a separate section. Some authors and international institutions (ILO, 2013; IMF, 2017; Kohler et al., 2019; Stockhammer, 2009, 2017) have highlighted financialisation as a central aspect. Financialisation is understood as the increasing influence of financial institutions and financial motives on economic activities. This aspect can work in several ways. The maximising shareholder value primacy has put pressure on firms to increase profits in the short term in order to improve dividends (ILO, 2011, 2013; Schwartz, 2021), which penalises labour by being done to the detriment of wages (Palladino, 2019) and productive investment and employment (ILO, 2011; Stockhammer, 2008; Schwartz, 2021). Financialisation has also weakened the bargaining power of workers through the previous mechanism and because firms have diversified their applications of capital and the locations of investments (Stockhammer, 2009), leading to an increase in multinational enterprises and, therefore, in competition between workers of the same firm sited in different locations. Moreover, often after having taken into account the maximising shareholder value, these firms have arbitrated between costs and rentabilities of different investments and locations, resulting in the creation of GVCs.

In economic policy, the shift towards supply-side policies since the 1980's has meant the reconfiguration of the wage as an economic variable. The wage has come to be viewed primarily as a variable that influences the cost of production rather than as an income component capable of ensuring high and stable flows of aggregate demand. The wage has thus become an adjustment variable, used as a policy instrument in anti-inflationary policies, in competitiveness policies, in employment policies and in the promotion of private investment. To support these ends, policies to make labour markets more flexible have been pursued, primarily in the European Union (Antunes, 2005, 2014). These policies have been behind the increase in non-standard employment adverted to above. Lavoie and Stockhammer (2012) classified them as pro-capital distributional policies, since they lead to a long-term decline in the labour income share by causing wage moderation. This moderation has been experienced essentially in the low- and middle-labour income groups and is thus a driver of labour market inequality.

3. Global Value Chains

3.1. A promising idea

Fostered by significant technological change and the widespread adoption of policies aimed at reducing trade costs, the rise and growth of GVCs – which already account for around half of world trade (World Bank, 2020) – have created the context for the countries of the Global South to converge to GDP per capita levels of the Global North (Dünhaupt & Herr, 2020). A positioning in global markets based on the production and export of natural resources (e.g. crude oil or coffee) creates a specialisation that deters developing countries from industrialising, while the division of production into different tasks, which are allocated all over the world, would offer these countries an opportunity to insert themselves into global production by exploring their comparative advantage in simple fabrication and by so promoting their industrialisation process. Also, the participation in GVCs will provide firms with an opportunity for acquiring better technology and know-how and forming trade networks (Gereffi, 2014). This line of reasoning has led international organisations like the World Bank to place a special emphasis on enabling developing countries to integrate GVCs as a means of achieving higher economic growth (World Bank, 2020).

Developing countries usually integrate themselves in low value--added activities, while developed countries operate either at the upstream or downstream end of the value chains, where maximum value addition takes place – a widely-accepted, empirically confirmed stylised fact, known as the smile curve (Rungi & Del Prete, 2018; Stöllinger, 2021). High value-added pre-fabrication tasks (e.g. research, design, logistics, and finance) and high value-added post-fabrication tasks (e.g. selling, marketing and high quality after sales services) in GVCs are taken over by developed countries. This production sharing divides production partners in GVCs into factory economies on the one hand and headquarter economies on the other hand (Baldwin & Lopez-Gonzalez, 2015), so bargaining power differences play an important role in the distribution of value added (Dindial et al., 2020).

As a rule, GVCs are governed by lead firms which in many cases are multinational enterprises, whose decisions to move offshore or to outsource are determined by profitability. Lead firms or big first--tier (or even second- or third-tier) suppliers can dictate the price of the task to their suppliers and set it to a level which minimises profits of these firms and the wages of their workers, increasing value-added differences between simple tasks and more sophisticated tasks and hindering investment possibilities besides inhibiting domestic demand in the developing countries. The upward move along the value chain, if not impossible (e.g. China), requires higher skills and innovation, together with property rights and knowledge-intensive intangible assets known as knowledge-based capital (Organisation for Economic Co-operation and Development [OECD], 2013). Thus, since countries with an abundant endowment of unskilled labour tend to occupy the labour-intensive functions of the value chain, they face a compressed development path that is dependent not just on their internal dynamics but also on the global business networks of which they are a part (Whittaker et al., 2010). External and internal economies of scale and technological leadership support each other and create high barriers for the catching-up of developing countries (Dünhaupt & Herr, 2020).

3.2. Labour market inequality

While integration in GVCs might help to generate more job opportunities through productivity and scale effects, trade in GVCs has given rise to a major global reallocation of jobs. In high income countries, technological change and exposure to trade with lower income countries contribute to the reallocation of value added from labour to capital. Inequality can also creep upward in the labour market, with a growing premium for skilled labour and stagnant wages for low- and middle-skilled labour (World Bank, 2020). Also, the relatively low-tech production stages that are less dependent on high-skilled labour have been transferred to developing countries. This reduces developed countries' relative demand for unskilled labour and causes an increase in average skill intensity in these countries (Ma et al., 2019). However, growth in skilled employment may create new jobs for less skilled workers, but accompanied by a decrease in unskilled average wages, particularly when controlling for increased house prices. The reduction of wages is caused by new entrants to the labour market, not by existing workers earning less (Lee & Clark, 2019).

Developing countries received the relatively low-tech production stages but, for these countries, it meant an upgrading of production processes and a need for the relatively more skilled labour than the average. Since GVC firms are more profitable, despite the conditions imposed by lead firms, they pay higher wages than non-GVC firms, and upgrading in the GVCs to the upstream sectors enlarges the wage inequality of skills (Wang et al., 2021). Thus, GVCs also impact the wage premium in developing countries, creating inequality in labour income.

4. A look ahead

At the start of this new decade, the global system of international production is experiencing a perfect storm, with the crisis caused by the COVID-19 pandemic arriving on top of existing challenges arising from the new industrial revolution (NIR), growing economic nationalism and the sustainability imperative (United Nations Conference on Trade and Development, 2020). Each in its own way, NIR technologies (robotics and artificial intelligence-enabled automation, enhanced supply chain digitalisation and additive manufacturing – 3D printing), which depend on industry-specific deployment, will flatten, squeeze or bend the "smile curve" of international production. Sustainability concerns, especially, will affect the business case for complex international production networks and will reshape GVCs. The transition to a circular economy will also foster production and consumption processes to be restructured causing a profound impact in value chain organisation (Nandi et al., 2021).

New technologies are set to drive future growth across industries and to increase the demand for new job roles and skill sets (World Economic Forum, 2020) as governments and societies will face unappealing choices, since climate change and environmental limits will make it harder to maintain and enhance global prosperity. Structural changes, such as the sudden upsurge in homeworking, will cause economic and social disruption, challenging existing labour market institutions. Labour market and unemployment policies will have to change in concert with a changing economy and move towards an understanding of the social as something always connected to the natural environment (Stamm et al., 2020).

Moreover, the investments required to achieve sustainability transitions and the redistribution needs entailed by this structural transformation will make it imperative to fight against the deleterious effects of tax evasion schemes and offshore tax havens. Ultimately, new public policies will emerge aiming to improve the ecological situation and to do so in a way that redistributes resources from upper to lower- and middle-income groups. However, the secondary distribution of income although necessary is not enough. Following Belser and Waziri, the priority must be primary distribution of income, since the necessary transitions cannot be made on supply-side alone. The demand side needs the capacity to respond with new consumptions and stimulus for the new investments.

References

Antunes, M. (2005), *O Desemprego na Política Económica – Uma reflexão sobre Portugal no Contexto da União Europeia*. Coimbra: Coimbra Editora.

Antunes, M. (2014), "Da estabilização macroeconómica às 'reformas estruturais': o papel do sistema de subsídio de desemprego europeu", *Boletim de Ciências Económicas – Homenagem ao Prof. Doutor António José Avelãs Nunes*, LVII (Tomo I), 453-491.

Atkinson, A. B., Piketty, T., & Saez, E. (2011), "Top incomes in the long run of history", *Journal of Economic Literature, 49*(1), 3-71. http:www.aeaweb.org/articles.php?doi=10.1257/jel.49.1.3

Baker, D., Bivens, J., & Schieder, J. (2019), *Reining in CEO compensation and curbing the rise of inequality* (Report). Economic Policy Institute. https://files.epi.org/pdf/168855.pdf

Baldwin, R., & Lopez⊠Gonzalez, J. (2015), "Supply⊠chain trade: A portrait of global patterns and several testable hypotheses", *The World Economy, 38*(11), 1682-1721. doi: 10.1111/twec.12189

Berman, Y., & Milanovic, B. (2020), *Homoploutia: Top Labor and Capital Incomes in the United States, 1950-2020.* (World Inequality Lab – Working Paper N° 2020/27). Wid.World. https://wid.world/document/homoploutia-top-labor-and-capital-incomes-in-the-united-states-1950-2020-world-inequality-lab-wp-2020-27/

Dindial, M., Clegg, J., & Voss, H. (2020), "Between a rock and a hard place: A critique of economic upgrading in global value chains", *Global Strategy Journal*, 10(3), 473-495. DOI: 10.1002/gsj.1382

Dünhaupt, P., & Herr, H. (2020), "Global value chains – a ladder for development?", *International Review of Applied Economics, 35*(3-4), 456-474. DOI: 10.1080/02692171.2020.1815665

European Commission (2007), "The labour income share in the European Union", In *Employment in Europe 2007*, 237-272.

Gereffi, G. (2014), "Global value chains in a post-Washington Consensus world", *Review of international political economy, 21*(1), 9-37. DOI: 10.1080/09692290.2012.756414

International Labour Organization (2008), "Trends in employment and inequality", In *Income Inequalities in the Age of Financial Globalization* (World of Work Report 2008), 1-37. https://www.ilo.org/wcmsp5/groups/public/---dgreports/---dcomm/---publ/documents/publication/wcms_100354.pdf

International Labour Organization (2011), "Making profits work for investment and jobs", In *Making markets work for jobs* (World of Work Report 2011), 31-53. https://www.ilo.org/wcmsp5/groups/public/---dgreports/---dcomm/---publ/documents/publication/wcms_166021.pdf

International Labour Organization (2013), "The fall in the labour income share", In *Wages and equitable growth* (Global Wage Report 2012/13), 41-53. https://www.ilo.org/wcmsp5/groups/public/---dgreports/---dcomm/---publ/documents/publication/wcms_194843.pdf

International Labour Organization (2016), *Non-standard Employment around the World – Understanding challenges, shaping prospects.* International Labour Office. https://www.ilo.org/wcmsp5/groups/public/---dgreports/---dcomm/---publ/documents/publication/wcms_534326.pdf

International Labour Organization (2021), *Inequalities and the World of Work* (ILC.109/Report IV(Rev.). https://www.ilo.org/wcmsp5/groups/public/---ed_norm/---relconf/documents/meetingdocument/wcms_792123.pdf

International Monetary Fund (2007), "The globalization of labor", In *World Economic Outlook – April 2007*, 161-192. https://www.imf.org/en/Publications/WEO/Issues/2016/12/31/Spillovers-and-Cycles-in-the-Global-Economy

International Monetary Fund (2017), "Understanding the Downward Trend in Labor Income Shares", In *World Economic Outlook – April 2017*, 121-172. https://www.elibrary.imf.org/view/books/081/23926-9781475564655-en/23926-9781475564655-en-book.xml

Kohler, K., Guschanski, A., & Stockhammer, E. (2019), "The impact of financialisation on the wage share: a theoretical clarification and empirical test", *Cambridge Journal of Economics*, *43*, 937-974. https://doi.org/10.1093/cje/bez021

Lavoie, M., & Stockhammer, E. (2012), *Wage-led growth: Concept, theories and policies* (Conditions of Work and employment Series No. 41). International Labour Office. International Labour Organization. https://www.ilo.org/wcmsp5/groups/public/---ed_protect/---protrav/---travail/documents/publication/wcms_192507.pdf

Lee, N., & Clarke, S. (2019), "Do low-skilled workers gain from high-tech employment growth? High-technology multipliers, employment and wages in Britain", *Research Policy*, *48*(9), 103803. https://doi.org/10.1016/j.respol.2019.05.012

Ma, S., Liang, Y., & Zhang, H. (2019), « The employment effects of global value chains", *Emerging Markets Finance and Trade*, *55*(10), 2230-2253. DOI: 10.1080/1540496X.2018.1520698

Mishel, L., & Schieder, J. (2018), CEO Compensation Surged in 2017. (Report). Economic Policy Institute. https://files.epi.org/pdf/152123.pdf

Nandi, S., Sarkis, J., Hervani, A. A., & Helms, M. M. (2021), "Redesigning supply chains using blockchain-enabled circular economy and COVID-19 experiences", *Sustainable Production and Consumption*, *27*, 10-22. https://doi.org/10.1016/j.spc.2020.10.019

Organisation for Economic Co-operation and Development (2013), "Knowledge-based capital and upgrading in global value chains", In *Supporting Investment in Knowledge Capital, Growth and Innovation*. Paris: OECD. https://doi.org/10.1787/9789264193307-9-en

Palladino, L. (2019), *Ending Shareholder Primacy in Corporate Governance* (Roosevelt Institute Working Paper). https://rooseveltinstitute.org/wp-content/uploads/2020/07/RI_EndingShareholderPrimacy_workingpaper_201902.pdf

Rodrik, D., & Stantcheva, S. (2021), "A Policy Matrix for Inclusive Prosperity (Policy Brief No. 30)", *Economics for Inclusive Prosperity*. https://j.mp/3aJwN7J

Rungi, A., & Del Prete, D. (2018), "The smile curve at the firm level: Where value is added along supply chains", *Economics Letters*, *164*, 38-42. https://doi.org/10.1016/j.econlet.2017.12.038

Schwartz, H. M. (2021), "Vampires at the Gate?: Finance and Slow Growth", *American Affairs*, *V*(4), 3-18. https://americanaffairsjournal.org/2021/11/vampires-at-the-gate-finance-and-slow-growth/

Stamm, I., Matthies, A. L., Hirvilammi, T., & Närhi, K. (2020), "Combining labour market and unemployment policies with environmental sustainability? A cross-national study on ecosocial innovations", *Journal of International and Comparative Social Policy*, *36*(1), 42-56. doi:10.1017/ics.2020.4

Stockhammer, E. (2008), "Some Stylized Facts on the Finance-dominated Accumulation Regime", *Competition & Change*, *12*(2), 184-202. DOI: 10.1179/102452908X289820

Stockhammer, E. (2009). *Determinants of Functional Income Distribution in OECD Countries* (IMK Studies 5/2009). IMK Macroeconomic Policy Institute. https://www.imk-boeckler.de/de/faust-detail.htm?sync_id=HBS-004499

Stockhammer, E. (2017), "Determinants of the wage share. A panel analysis of advanced and developing economies", *British Journal of Industrial Relations*, 55(1), 3-33. https://doi.org/10.1111/bjir.12165

Stöllinger, R. (2021), "Testing the smile curve: functional specialisation and value creation in GVCs", *Structural Change and Economic Dynamics*, 56, 93-116. https://doi.org/10.1016/j.strueco.2020.10.002

United Nations Conference on Trade and Development (2020), *World investment report 2020: International production beyond the pandemic.* https://unctad.org/system/files/official-document/wir2020_en.pdf

Wang, S., He, Y., & Song, M. (2021), "Global value chains, technological progress, and environmental pollution: Inequality towards developing countries", *Journal of Environmental Management*, 277, 110999. https://doi.org/10.1016/j.strueco.2020.10.002

Whittaker, D. H., Zhu, T., Sturgeon, T., Tsai, M. H., & Okita, T. (2010), "Compressed development", *Studies in Comparative International Development*, 45(4), 439-467. DOI 10.1007/s12116-010-9074-8

World Bank (2020), *World Development Report 2020: Trading for Development in the Age of Global Value Chains.* Washington, DC: World Bank. doi:10.1596/978-1-4648-1457-0

World Economic Forum (2020), *The future of jobs report.* October. https://www3.weforum.org/docs/WEF_Future_of_Jobs_2020.pdf

CHAPTER 6:
WHAT LIES BEHIND GENDER PAY GAPS?
THE ILO GLOBAL WAGE REPORT 2018/19[100]

Catarina Braga[101]

1. Introduction

Target 8.5 of UN Sustainable Development Goal (SDG) number 8 reads: "By 2030, achieve full and productive employment and decent work for all women and men, including for young people and persons with disabilities, and equal pay for work of equal value." The present paper offers a summary of some of the key aspects covered by the International Labour Organization's (ILO) *Global Wage Report 2018/19*, which aims to measure gender pay gaps by means of an innovative methodology designed to understand what lies behind those gaps.

2. Main wage trends

According to the *ILO Global Wage Report 2018/19*, global wage growth in 2017 decreased to its lowest rate since 2008 and re-

---

[100] This paper was received in February 2020 (originally in Portuguese language) and corresponds to the author's participation in the seminar "Wage Report/Gender Pay Gap" (2nd edition of "Cátedra OIT/ILO Chair"), held at the University of Coimbra, Faculty of Economics (FEUC), on February 21, 2019.

[101] Specialist in labour relations and collective bargaining at the headquarters of the International Labour Organization, in Geneva. She belongs to the Unit for Inclusive Labour Markets, Labour Relations and Working Conditions (INWORK), ILO.

https://doi.org/10.14195/978-989-26-2277-4_11

mained well below the levels that had obtained before the global financial crisis. In real terms – i.e., adjusted for inflation –, global wage growth fell from 2.4% in 2016 to a mere 1.8% in 2017. If we do not count China, the sheer size of which gives it a huge impact and where wages have gone up at a very fast pace, global wage growth would have been even lower.

Despite the recovery in GDP growth and the steady decrease in unemployment rates, wage growth in high-income countries was slow in 2017, something which has been the subject of debate. Multiple explanations of the fact have been put forward, including slow productivity growth, greater global competition, workers' loss of bargaining power as new technologies are being adopted, the fact that unemployment statistics fail to adequately capture slack in the labour market,[102] and also economic uncertainty, which has probably caused companies to refrain from raising wages. Other possible explanations point to a shift to more capital-intensive industries, or higher capital intensity within industries.

3. Wage growth below productivity growth in high-income countries

Based on an analysis of existing trends in average wages and labour productivity in 52 high-income countries during the period 1999-2017, the Report finds that, on average, labour productivity increased faster (17%) than real wages (13%), even if the difference between the two trends decreased between 2015 and 2017. Overall, the decoupling of wages and labour productivity explains why labour income as a proportion of GDP remains, in many countries, below

---

[102] Labour market slack comprises what are known as "discouraged" workers – in other words, workers who remain unemployed but are no longer mentioned in unemployment statistics – and those who work fewer hours than they would like. These two realities are part of an unemployment rate that is probably underestimated.

that of the early 1990s. The ILO has emphasised this very aspect in previous editions of its *Global Wage Report*. The slowdown in labour productivity may help explain the slow wage growth in high-income economies, but it is unlikely that this is the only explanation.

Based on data from 64 countries that, together, account for about 75% of the world's wage employees, and using the Gini coefficient, the 2018/19 Report finds that the countries with the lowest rates of wage inequality are in the high-income group. Portugal is included in this group as the third most unequal country, after Chile and Latvia.

Based on data from 73 countries corresponding to about 80% of those employed in the world, the Report uses four different combinations (mean/median and hourly/monthly wages) to estimate the gender pay gap. It should be pointed out that the two measures that are most commonly used to measure the wage differential are the mean gender pay gap – that is, the difference between the average of all the wages earned by women and the average of all the wages earned by men – and the median gender pay gap, which compares the value located in the middle of the women's wage distribution with the value located in the middle of the men's wage distribution. Both the mean and median gender pay gaps can also be calculated based on monthly or hourly wages.

The first point that needs to be made is that, regardless of which of the four combinations is used, men earn more than women. The Report finds that, using average hourly wages (as suggested by indicator 8.5.1 of the UN Sustainable Development Goals), the global gender pay gap stands at around 16%, whereas if we use median monthly wages, women earn approximately 22% less than men globally. The second point that needs to be made is that, for almost all countries – notably Portugal –, the gender pay gap is higher when the estimate is based on monthly rather than hourly wages, a fact that has to do with the issue of working time. In fact, using hourly wages – as opposed to monthly wages – to calculate the gender pay gap has the advantage of disentangling the number of hours worked from earnings. In other words, regardless of the number of hours worked, it is always possible to determine what the payment per hour is. Using other measures – wages paid on a monthly, weekly or daily basis – can reflect differences not only in hourly pay but also in the number of hours worked over a certain period of time. The third observation is that, in the case of many countries, the mean and median gender pay gap can yield very different results even if the same pay definition – i.e., monthly or hourly earnings – is used. As regards Portugal, the Report finds that the gender pay gap ranges from 16 to 20%, depending on which measure is being used. The highest gender pay gap (approximately 20%) is obtained by using median monthly wages.

4. The Report's innovative methodology

The Report analyses the reasons for the gaps detected by the various measures used and proposes an innovative methodology that makes it possible to arrive at a complementary measure: the factor-weighted gender pay gap. In the majority of countries, female participation in wage employment has distinct characteristics, with women tending to cluster around specific wage brackets. To put it differently, male and female workers are not evenly distributed across the wage distribution. Thus, conventional wage gap estimates based on a single value – whether the mean or the median – provide information that is of limited use for policy-makers. Portugal, where a large share of women are paid the minimum wage, is a case in point. In fact, at the median the hourly wage for Portuguese women is close to the minimum wage, which suggests that a very significant number of women are paid close to the minimum wage. However, the average hourly wage for Portuguese women is much higher than the median hourly wage. The reason is that there are small groups of women workers in higher wage brackets, and, given that the average hourly wage is thus pushed higher for all women, this ends up skewing the result and causes the mean-based gender pay gap to be lower. The ILO's new methodology for estimating factor-weighted gender pay gaps makes it possible to take into account the weight of those small groups of better-paid women within the workforce as a whole, as the subgroup in question will now be weighted based on its representativeness *vis-à-vis* the total number of workers. This will prevent that subgroup of relatively better-paid women from skewing the mean.

In short, the new methodology groups male and female wage employees into homogeneous subgroups, based on four factors. It then estimates the gender pay gap in each subgroup based on the mean or the median. Finally, a weighted average of the estimated gender pay gaps of all the subgroups is constructed, with weights reflecting the size of each subgroup in the total population of wage employees. The four factors on the basis of which the total population of wage employees was grouped into homogeneous subgroups are the following: i) "education"; ii) "age" (as a proxy for work experience); iii) working hours and iv) "private-sector or public-sector employment". The human capital model[103] provides the basis for the two factors 'education' and 'experience' in the labour market, which are two important indicators as far as the employment profile of employees is concerned. It is also a fact that the participation of women and men in the labour market tends to differ in terms of hours of work, hence the choice of working time as the third factor. It is also the case that in almost all countries

---

103 Mincer, J. (1974), Schooling, experience, and earnings (New York, NY, National Bureau of Economic Research Press). See page 37 of the *ILO Global Wage Report 2018/19*.

for which data is available, women are more likely than men to work in the public sector rather than the private sector, hence the choice of this last dimension.

Figure 1 (which reproduces page 44 of the *Global Wage Report 2018/19*, see below) compares raw gender pay gaps and factor- -weighted gender pay gaps – i.e., i) the difference in average wages between all women and all men who are engaged in paid employment and ii) that same difference when we apply the new methodology proposed by the ILO, respectively. In both cases hourly wages have been used. We can see that, in the majority of countries under analysis, the factor-weighted gender pay gap (red dot) is higher than the raw gender pay gap (yellow bar). It is also possible to conclude that, worldwide (blue bar), the gender pay differential increases from about 16% to 19% when our estimate is based on factor-weighted gender pay gaps rather than on raw gender pay gaps.

An interesting finding, and one that lends a lot of credibility to the new methodology proposed by the ILO, is that the mean and median factor-weighted gender pay gaps are closer in value than in the classic measures of gender pay gaps. This is a clear improvement, given that opting for mean or median is often a subjective choice, with implications in terms of policy-making.

Figure 1: Comparing raw gender pay gaps and factor-weighted gender pay gaps using mean hourly wage in both cases: Classification based on ranking countries (within five groups) by raw gender pay gap (Reproduction of p. 44, *Global Wage Report* 2018/1)

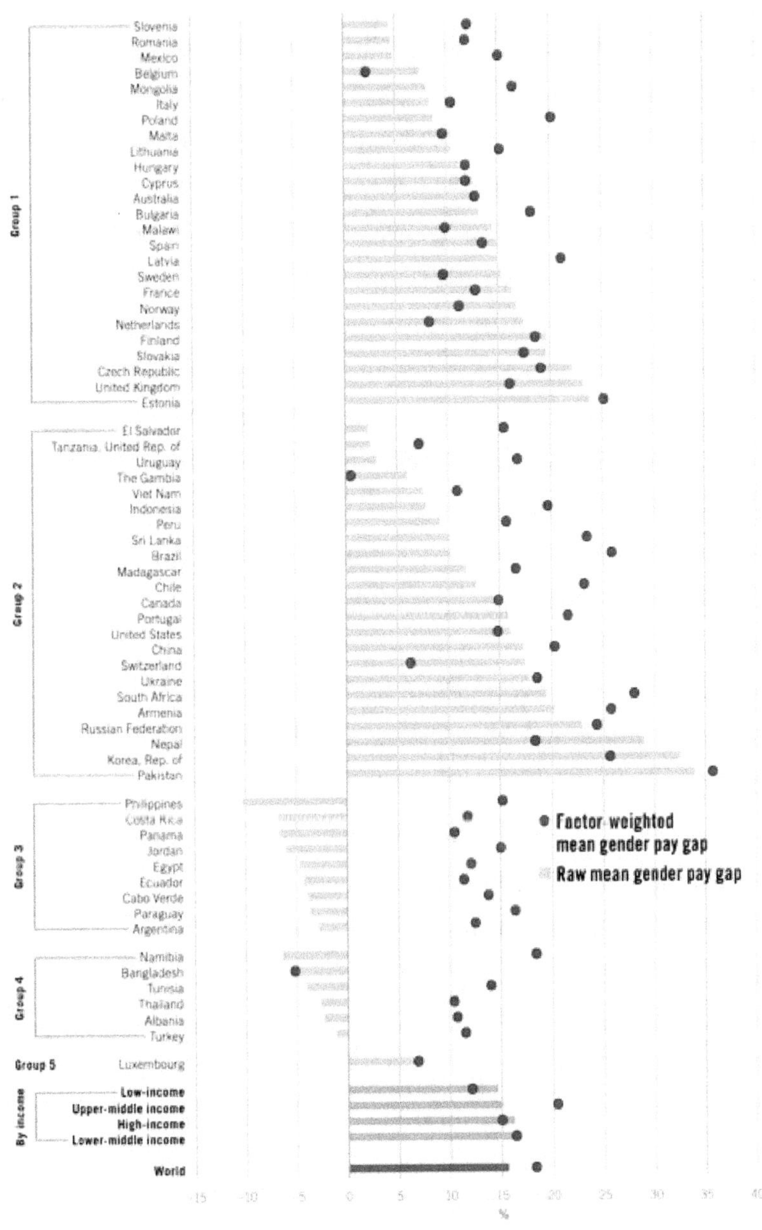

Source: ILO estimates combining the gender pay gaps from figure 14 (bars) and figure 19 (dots).

5. What are the factors behind the gender pay gap?

In order to understand this phenomenon, we have to measure it in each wage bracket. With that in mind, the Report estimates the gender pay gap at different points in the hourly wage distribution, i.e., at each of the nine deciles that split the distribution into ten equally sized groups. The analysis moves from the first decile, which corresponds to the wage value separating the lowest--paid 10% of workers (meaning that 90% of the observed wages are higher than that) to the ninth decile, which corresponds to the cut-off point for the highest-paid 10% (meaning that 90% of the observed wages are lower). Estimating gender pay gaps at different points in the wage distribution is bound to yield more information than is the case with a single, simple measure, and is potentially relevant in that it allows measures to be adjusted so as to increase policy effectiveness. In addition, the Report estimates the proportion of women in the various wage brackets, with the aim of determining the extent to which they are over--represented in the lowest wage brackets or under-represented in the highest ones.

Regardless of a country's income level, the fact is that a common pattern can be detected in labour markets across the world: as one moves from lower to higher hourly wages, the proportion of women decreases, in some cases sharply. Take, for example, Portugal, where approximately three quarters of the lowest-paid 10% of workers are women. In high-income countries, the wage pay gap tends to widen at the upper end of the distribution. To put it differently, although the "sticky floor" and the "glass ceiling" effects can be felt in these countries, the latter is far more prominent, even if on average it may affect fewer women.

6. The Report's next step was to decompose the "explained" and "unexplained" parts of the gender pay gap

The "explained" part is that portion of the gender pay gap that can be attributed to differences inherent in the worker (age, education, years of experience), job attributes (working time, occupational categories) and workplace characteristics (company size, type of activity, public or private sector, geographical location). As to the "unexplained" part, it is the part with which we are left after taking into account all the factors that could objectively contribute to determine the wages of women and men. The aim here is basically to try to understand whether men earn more than women because – for example – they are better educated or because they possess other observable characteristics or skills associated with higher labour productivity. This breakdown of the gender pay gap has a number of advantages. Decomposing the gender pay gap in this manner offers a number of benefits. First, it helps identify that part of the gender pay gap which can be explained by differences in educational attainment and it may prove useful in helping decision-makers when it comes, for example, to designing policies aimed at diversifying schooling and training options, thereby encouraging girls to move into less traditional areas. Second, if the size of the unexplained component is large, it could mean that reducing the gender pay gap will require measures aimed at eliminating pay discrimination as well as the fostering of legal frameworks and policies conducive to equal pay for work of equal value for women and men. In this connection, an exercise is conducted in which the explanatory factor of education has been isolated in some of the analyses, so that a decomposition is effected that results in the following three parts: "explained by education", "explained by factors other than education", and "unexplained".

The analysis leads to the conclusion that in most countries, regardless of their income level, the gender pay gap remains mostly unexplained by specific characteristics and differences between men and women. Generally speaking, in high-income countries, differences in education have only a residual role in explaining the gender pay gap. In cases where education explains part of the existing gap, most often than not it is because it contributes to bridging rather than widening it. This is not surprising, given that in the countries in question women employees are better educated than men.

7. Understanding what lies behind the "unexplained" part of the gender pay gap

7.1. The wages of women and men in the same occupation

With regard to the underlying reasons for the "unexplained" part of the gender pay gap, the report conducts an analysis of occupational categories and shows that in many countries women earn lower wages than men within the same occupational categories despite having higher levels of education. This demonstrates that women tend to have lower wage returns for their education than men, even when they work in the same occupational category.

7.2. Wages in female-dominated occupations

Another part of the answer has to do with the undervaluation of women's work in highly feminised occupations and companies. In this regard, the Report shows that the wages of men and women with similar levels of education tend to be lower in female-dominated occupations than in other occupations.

7.3. Wages in companies with a predominantly female workforce

The Report also seeks to determine the effect a predominantly female workforce has on the average wages paid by companies. The findings show that the average wages of highly feminised companies – more specifically, companies in which 65% or more of the workers are women – are substantially lower than the average wages estimated for all the companies that share the same profile. On the other hand, in companies with a predominantly male workforce, the average wage is higher than in companies that share the same profile. In order to make sure that the companies covered by the Report were truly comparable, they were selected based on such aspects as size/number of employees, economic sector, region, whether they were public or private, and the type of collective bargaining agreement under which their employees work, regardless of whether the workforce is predominantly male or female. In other words, one can in fact conclude that differences in productivity cannot be the only reason why predominantly female companies pay lower wages. One hypothesis may be that the labour income share received by workers in these companies is low compared to what workers earn in male-dominated companies. If this is true, it would imply that there is less value attached to labour in highly feminised companies, even though the value of the work and production these companies bring to society may be comparable to those of other companies in sectors traditionally dominated by male workers.

7.4. The effects of parenthood status on wages

Finally, the Report analyses the motherhood pay gap and the fatherhood pay gap, defined as the pay gap between mothers and non-mothers and the pay gap between fathers and non-fathers, respectively. Lower wages for mothers may have to do with a number of factors, including career breaks, reductions in working time, employment in more family-friendly jobs which are lower-paying – usually in the public sector or in jobs requiring shorter working hours –, or stereotypical hiring and promotion decisions at company level, which end up penalising the careers of working mothers. The general conclusion is that mothers are faced with a wage penalty. The data available for most countries suggests that from age 25-35 onwards – that being the age range during which, on average, women begin having children –, women's participation in the labour market is significantly affected compared to that of men. This, in turn, has an impact on wages, and this not just a short-term effect, given that it has relatively long-term consequences for a significant percentage of women across the world, including consequences for their contributory careers.

8. Implications of/on a series of policies

The gender pay gap does not seem to be explainable by any of the objective factors that are usually associated with the determination of wages. Differences in educational attainment are only marginally important in explaining the pay gap, not least because women are better educated than men. Thus, in view of the fact that women are not paid in accordance with these objective factors, the gender pay gap seems to be underestimated.

The report finds that in many countries the most significant part of the gender pay gap cannot be explained by differences in education attainment nor by such factors as age, experience, occupational category, or the sector of the economy in which one works. A number of studies argue that part of the unexplained gender pay gap is the result of discrimination against women in relation to men. That is the case whenever women earn less than men for the same work or for work of equal value. Direct wage discrimination includes cases in which two jobs that are the same have different titles, depending on the gender of the person performing them, and are paid differently, with men typically being paid higher wages than women. Examples include the titles of "chef" for men versus "cook" for women, "information manager" versus "librarian", and "management assistant" versus "secretary". There is also discrimination whereby women are paid less than men for work of equal value, i.e., work that may differ with regard to the specific tasks, responsibilities, knowledge, skills and effort involved or the conditions under which it is performed, but which ultimately is of equal worth. Indirect wage discrimination is more subtle, and therefore harder to detect. It may manifest itself in a variety of practices, including, for example, in the way in which wages are structured and the relative weight in overall remuneration of seniority or of bonuses for long hours of continued presence in the workplace.

Wages are widely recognised as a fundamental determinant of household income – in other words, of aggregate demand and inclusive growth. The issue of slow wage growth, which is duly highlighted in the present Report, has been repeatedly described as a source of concern and is now part of the international political agenda. It is therefore imperative to have a better grasp of the role that wage policies can play in ensuring a better fit between wage growth and productivity growth in those countries where there has been a decoupling in the trends of these two variables. It is also relevant to find out how better coordination at the international level might be used to promote sustainable wage growth that proves capable of supporting aggregate demand at the national, regional and global level. More and more countries are focusing on domestic legislation prohibiting pay discrimination against women and on measures aimed at promoting equal pay between women and men.

However, while 40% of the world's countries have fully adopted the principle of "equal pay for work of equal value", the remaining countries have chosen to focus on the narrower principle of "equal pay for equal work".

Some countries have taken steps to foster pay transparency, so as to bring to light differentials between women and men. For that purpose, they require (usually large) companies to disclose the earnings of their employees. In recent years, a number of countries have embraced proactive pay equity laws that require employers to look regularly into their compensation practices, assess the gender pay gaps, and take action to eliminate the portion of the gap that is caused by discrimination in pay. Thus, for example, since 2018, German companies with 200 or more wage employees are required to disclose the earnings of their employees, whether men or women, on demand to any employee who requests it. By the same token, in the United Kingdom, since April 2017, every company and public sector organisation with 250 or more employees is required to publish data on the difference between mean and median wages and bonuses, as well as the gender pay gap at different pay scales. If Swiss employers with 50 employees or more wish to participate in public tenders, they are required to carry out a pay audit and remove the discriminatory part of the pay difference. In Iceland, since January 2018, companies and government agencies with more than 25 employees must obtain government certification from an independent entity attesting to the fact that their pay policies are gender-equal.

In Portugal, the 2019 law determining measures to promote equal pay between women and men for the same work or for work of equal value brought several changes centred around four key aspects: more information, greater transparency, a presumption of pay discrimination in cases where employees claim that they are being discriminated against and their employers fail to prove that they have a transparent remuneration policy in place, and a strengthening of the powers of the Authority for Working Conditions (ACT) and the Commission for Equality in Labour and Employment (CITE). One of the tools introduced by the new legislation was the Gender Pay Gap Barometer, which is aimed at promoting more and better data on the country's gender pay gap.

Gender pay gap reporting exposes the size of the gender pay gap, thereby helping detect possible cases of pay discrimination. Equal pay audits are another key tool. They help determine which factors drive pay, and may therefore prove useful in identifying possible flaws in a company's pay practices. Countries should also seek ways to address the undervaluing of women's work in highly feminised occupations and industries, including by raising wages in the professions and sectors in question. Removing this bias is not only a way to reducing the gender pay gap but also a precondition for reducing occupational segregation, e.g. by drawing more men into such sectors as education and health.

Some of the choices women make and some of their expectations may be the product of enduring gender-based stereotypes and imbalances in unpaid work related to child and elderly care and to housework in general. Women would be in a better position to make different occupational choices if family duties were shared more equitably between men and women and if adequate childcare and elderly care services were made available. Adequate company policies regarding flexible working-time arrangements would also make a difference. The lack of programmes to support women's return to work after maternity leave also contributes to the wage penalty with which they are faced when resuming work after a prolonged period of absence from the labour market. Increasing the right of men to parental leave would also help to rebalance the perception of working mothers held by their employers.

Given that the factors that drive and explain gender pay gaps vary not only from one country to the next but also in different parts of the distribution, the measures required to reduce them also need to be country-specific. One of the findings of this Report is that better data on the distribution of wages is needed, particularly as far as low- and middle-income countries are concerned. In countries where these data are not yet collected but where there already exist surveys on employment or something similar, question modules, aimed at addressing aspects identified as potential determinants of the gender pay gap, can be designed and tested, thereby clearly and specifically linking, for instance, the existence of children to each individual female or male worker in the household. Furthermore, panel data collection, which makes it possible to track the same person over time, can prove important in terms of solving certain of the issues related to the interpretation of life-cycle events.

Mean- or median-based estimates of the gender pay gap provide a raw measurement of the wage dispersion of the employed population. These are well-known indicators, and they have been useful in terms of attracting the attention of the general public and policy- -makers to the problem of unequal pay between women and men. Still, they may be insufficient in cases where female participation in the labour market is low and where women are disproportionately concentrated in specific sectors or occupational categories. Hence the Report's recommendation to look beyond raw measurements and analyse in more detail the wage structures of women and men according to more homogeneous subgroups, weighted by factors like education, years of experience, job characteristics and work- place characteristics.

It is crucial to know whether the gender pay gap in a given country is mostly driven by pay gaps at the bottom, in the middle, or at the top of the wage distribution, because that determination has important policy implications. Thus, for example, the introduction of minimum wage legislation could reduce the gender pay gap at lower wage levels. Furthermore, collective agreements with the potential to be extended to wider groups of workers could achieve the same effect, only higher up in the wage distribution. According to numerous studies, countries with a higher incidence of collective bargaining tend to have less wage inequality in general and, consequently, smaller gender pay gaps. In fact, collective agreements can make the reduction of this differential a prime objective by addressing a variety of issues in the first place: reconciling professional, personal and family life; increasing the transparency of company pay differentials; increasing the wages in female-dominated job categories; and using gender-neutral job evaluations aimed at ascertaining the relative value of such jobs – including of a different content – and at making sure that remuneration is fair. Finally, policies and measures that promote greater representation of women in senior and highly paid positions could have a positive effect in terms of reducing the gender pay gap at the top of the wage distribution. Measures aimed at fostering the formalisation of the informal economy can also greatly benefit women, by providing them with legal and effective protection and empowering them to better defend their own interests.

9. To conclude

The decomposition of the gender pay gap shows that part of it can be explained by differences in the employee's labour market attributes or by the characteristics inherent in a job or a workplace, notably the fact that women tend to work in occupations or industry sectors that pay less. However, saying that part of the gap can be explained is not the same as saying that it is "admissible". In fact, the concentration of women in certain sectors can be the result of existing stereotypes or social norms. Of course, the importance of these factors varies from one country to another.

Where women in paid employment have lower educational achievements than men, educational policies targeting enrolment rates among girls may contribute to reducing the gender pay gap in the future. In addition, reducing polarisation and occupational segregation may require changing perceptions and stereotypes, for example to attract more women into the areas of science, technology, engineering and mathematics (STEM), which offer better-paid employment opportunities, or to combat employer prejudice in hiring and/or promotion decisions. By the same token, occupational concentration and segregation may be countered by making jobs usually held by women more attractive to men.

We need to speed up the closing of the gender pay gap by building on the growing awareness of and commitment to gender equality that currently exist in the world of work and in society at large. A few general considerations need to be made in addition to the specific measures discussed above. First of all, speeding up the process will require both political commitment and social change. Although public policies aimed at improving education, social protection, protection at work, and the social infrastructure are necessary in order to close the gender pay gap, the effectiveness of such policies will hinge, at least in part, on shifting social norms and gender stereotypes. Some of these stereotypes are deeply rooted, regardless of the country's income level. Second, if we are to beat the gender pay gap we will need comprehensive, cross-cutting approaches to gender equality. The truth is that, as an indicator, the gender pay gap also captures many of the disadvantages faced by girls and women, both within and outside the labour market. Many countries have created gender equality commissions at the national level. Portugal's CITE is an example. Such commissions are expected to be based on social dialogue and to ensure direct participation on the part of social partners. Third, one cannot emphasise enough that finding the appropriate combination of policies in any national context will depend on the country's specific situation, and that robust analytical work will be required to identify the key contributing factors – and hence the most effective remedies – in each particular context.

COMMENT:

THE GENDER PAY GAP – A MUCH-DEBATED SYNTHETIC INDICATOR OF GENDER INEQUALITIES

Virgínia Ferreira[104] and Mónica Lopes[105]

Introduction

As a synthetic indicator of the existing inequalities between men and women, the gender pay gap is continuously monitored and scrutinised. More than seventy years ago, this differential became, in Europe, a phenomenon to be fought with public policies (Convention no. 100, of 1951; art. 141 of the Treaty of Rome, of 1957), and since then, it has been systematically calculated and highlighted, during which time it has been slow to develop (Ferreira, 2010; Cardoso et al., 2016). In fact, there are those who see its evolution as having become all but stagnant in the last two decades, especially in regard to those aspects of the pay gap that cannot be attributed to objective factors.

The data from the last four decades show that the stagnation of this gap, whether in respect of basic salary or earnings (including bonuses, overtime, or awards), is a global trend (Ferreira, 2010; Cardoso et al., 2016). An additional concern is the fact that some

---

[104] University of Coimbra, Faculty of Economics, Centre for Social Studies.

[105] University of Coimbra, Centre for Social Studies.

https://doi.org/10.14195/978-989-26-2277-4_12

patterns have been maintained or even accentuated – as is the case with the size of the pay gap in workers with the highest levels of education and at the top of professional hierarchies (Ferreira, 2010; Casaca, 2021).

The need to hasten the removal of the gender pay gap has given rise to a number of new methodologies for calculating it and policies to combat it. The methods of calculation differ depending on the assumptions on which they are based, with public policies aimed at eradication pointing in different directions according to the results obtained. The new methodology proposed in the ILO's initiative, as it is presented by Catarina Braga, aligns with this orientation.

There are different methodologies for measuring gender pay gaps. This diversity of calculation methods leads to challenges to the very idea that these gaps exist. It is argued that they are simply the effect of the calculation methods used, or that they derive from some illegal discriminatory practices. Moreover, it is added that the unexplained part in the various models will be determined by uncontrolled variables. Hence the announcements, often bearing more or less resounding titles – such as Kilgour's "The Gender-Based Pay Gap Is Gone" (2020) – that they have all but disappeared. It is useful, briefly (given restrictions imposed by the tight limits of this text), to understand why the positions in this debate are so pola-rized and, above all, the contrasting results of scientific research.

Pay gap value depends on the perspectives and methodolo-gies employed

The formulae for calculating the unadjusted or raw gender pay gap, based on the comparison of the mean or median wages of women and men in the total number of employees in the employed population, do not provoke much debate. This ceases to be the case when calculating the adjusted gap. Different understandings of the term 'remuneration' can be a source of divergence. As Rubery and Grimshaw (2014) express it (going back to Figart et al., 2002), remuneration can be seen as "wages as a price, wages as a living and wages as a social practice". The authors highlight the highly important role played by feminist criticism in the construction of the third perspective, emphasising the issue of the practices of agents, specifically employers. The feminist perspective made it visible that these practices were linked to gender ideologies and stereotypes, and not simply derived from the logic of the market, as neoclassical economics suggests, or from the principles of political economy, as proposed by Marxist economics. Thus, many of the discordances are a consequence of the different perspectives adopted to analyse the phenomenon: economic, sociological, institutional and organisational.

Early efforts to explain the gender pay gap employed a "human capital" model. This theory has been developed mainly from the work of the American economist G. S. Becker (1993), who argued that, as women tend to be less involved in employment and to invest fewer resources in education and training, they do not reap rewards commensurate with those of men in the labour market. Following on from the human capital approach, it has been popular to 'decompose' and quantify the influence of a range of observable characteristics, such as education and age, on the gender pay gap and the extent to which this explains the gap. This approach attempts to identify the core elements responsible for the difference between male and female pay. These analyses will provide a measure of the level of the gap that is 'explainable' with the unexplainable element often evaluated as resulting from unobservable factors such as discrimination.

However, since Becker made his analysis there has been an incisive reduction in the importance of education and experience in explanations of the gender pay gap, as women today have higher levels of schooling than men and are no longer interrupting their careers as often. Today the economic perspective focuses on: educational choices; unassessed productivity differences; the career orientation deficit; the lack of professional choices that ensure better work-family balance; increasing uncertainty in respect of the return guaranteed by investment in higher education, explained by the change in skills associated with technological transformation; the role of employer power, formerly underestimated, for example in the compression of wages; and unequal income distribution (Rubery & Grimshaw, 2014, 4).

In a sociological perspective – i.e., where the individual no longer takes centre stage –, the focus shifts to the pressure exerted by the culture of presenteeism in the workplace and to the processes of segregation and segmentation within the professions. Institutionally, the breakdown of the system of collective bargaining, the polarisation of wages, the growing proportion of women and men who are on the minimum wage, the reduction of remuneration in recognition of skills gained through experience, and the impact of the new public management on compression of wages and on the freezing of career progressions are all seen as significant.

Finally, in the remuneration policies of organisations there is a shift from setting a wage for each job to remuneration based on the profile of the person who occupies the job and the respective individual performance, often measured by questionable criteria. This translates into the individualisation of remuneration and is increasingly subject to the discretion of employers. Hence the relevance of the question "What is more important – what you do, where you do it, or who you are?" (Ferreira, 2010: 170).

It is important to recognise the contrasting effects of these trends – as women acquire more qualifications and have increasingly continuous trajectories of employment, opportunities for career advancement decrease. This is the result of an increase in temporary work, precariousness and the outsourcing of functions, for these are processes whose impact is mostly felt in female-dominated sectors of activity.

These considerations justify the by now longstanding words of Paula England and Peter Lewin:

"Economists and sociologists differ markedly in their views of discrimination. While sociological theory suggests mechanisms through which discrimination will persist and disadvantages caused by discrimination will be perpetuated, neoclassical economic theory suggests that market forces cause the demise of discrimination in the long run. These divergences in view have policy implications, with sociologists likely to favor governmental and other collective action, while economists are likely to see competitive markets as the best antidote" (emphasis in original) (1989: 239).

All methodologies have advantages and limitations

In this context, it is understandable that we should find different approaches leading to different points of view and different prescriptions for political action. The singularity of the methodology proposed by the ILO resides in the fact that it estimates the gender pay gap based on the weight given to each homogeneous subgroup of workers, defined according to four criteria: i) education; ii) age (as a proxy for work experience); iii) working time and iv) the public or private sector. By using hourly, as opposed to monthly or annual, remuneration it hopes to rule out the undue influence of the number of hours worked. The choice of the most appropriate unit is determined by the most common remuneration practices. For certain societies, annual remuneration will make more sense – that being the case, for instance, in the US, where the payment of annual bonuses is very common. In the case of Portugal, the conclusions reached by this ILO methodology are not very different from those produced by other methodologies. From these conclusions we note the following:

> a) The factor-weighted gender pay gap is higher than that obtained from the mean wages of men and women and it is higher in the group with the highest wages; these results tally with those of all other known and tested methodologies (González, 2010; Ferreira, 2010).
>
> b) Breaking down men's and women's wages according to individual attributes, the specifics of jobs and the characteristics of the workplaces leaves a large part of the pay gap unexplained (González 2010).
>
> c) The wages of women and men with similar levels of education tend to be lower in predominantly female companies or occupational categories (i.e. companies or categories with a 65% or more rate of feminisation); it has long been proved that wages are much lower in companies with a predominantly female workforce, something which has recently been confirmed by Card, Cardoso & Kline (2016).
>
> d) Women with children are penalised in terms of wages (Ferreira and Lopes, 2009).

We also find that results differ depending on the methods of decomposition employed. One that is widely used, for example in the study recently carried out as part of the project "The social and economic benefits of rewarding equality between women and men" (Casaca, 2021), is that of Oaxaca–Blinder, to which a number of limitations have also been pointed out. One such is the widely cited "index number problem". Since the choice of reference group can affect the ratio between the explained and unexplained parts of the gender pay gap, the value of the explained part of the pay gap will be different if we choose men's or women's wages as a reference. Another limitation of the Oaxaca-Blinder decomposition is that it can be difficult to make inferences about the main cause of the unexplained part of the gap. In short, each decomposition method has its own inherent assumptions, advantages and limitations.

The legislative framework in Portugal

In recent years, following the directives and guidelines of international, and specifically European, agencies, Portugal has strengthened legislation to combat wage inequality between women and men. In this context, particular emphasis should be given to Law No. 60/2018, of 21 August, which sought to reinforce transparency in remuneration practices. Under the new law, all companies are required to have a transparent compensation policy based on an objective evaluation of employee jobs, which accounts for differences related to productivity, merit pay, attendance record and seniority. Employers with 250 or more employees must submit an annual assessment of their gender pay gap, an action plan for eliminating the gap during the following year, and a report on their progress in fulfilling the previous year's plan. The assessment and plan must be submitted within 120 days of the Labour Authority's publication of the pay gap data. In the annual progress report, organisations must set out justified salary differences and the reduction of un-justified pay gaps. Gender pay differences that are not corrected or justified will be presumed to be discriminatory. Companies will face penalties for noncompliance and a two-year ban on tendering for public contracts. Companies with more than 50 employees are also expected to be covered by the law from 2022 on.

As provided for in Law No. 60/2018, in 2019 the Office of Statistics and Planning of Portugal's Ministry of Labour, Solidarity and Social Security (GEP/MTSSS) began publishing the Gender Pay Gap Barometer, based on the records of staff establishments. Because information provided by companies is not yet available, this is the most visible result so far of the new regulatory framework of 2018.

This normative text anticipates some of the provisions of the proposal for a Directive of the European Parliament and of the Council on salary transparency, aimed at strengthening the application of the principle of equal pay through a set of binding measures in the areas of transparency and the adoption of supervisory mechanisms to ensure their enforcement.

It can, therefore, be said that there is a tendency for policy to reinforce the obligation of transparency in remuneration practices. The Portuguese case is of considerable interest, since mandatory disclosure in the workplace and reporting by employers to the appropriate authorities of salary information has long been included in the national legislative framework, without producing the desired results. The information was, indeed, individualised and had to be verified by those working in the company, counting with a period of 15 days to detect anomalies. Trade unions, workers' committees and organisations representing employers could request access up to 10 days before the deadline for submission to the Labour Inspection (cf. Dec.-Law no. 479/76, updated by the Labour Code, Law no. 7 /2009). These provisions are retained in the new law but with slight changes. However, it has to be recognised that they haven't been effective. Let us hope that when this problem is placed on political, government and union agendas, the pressure on employers will finally produce results. Figures on the pay gap between men and women will probably continue to be the object of contestations that may be more or less inconsistent with the methodologies that gave rise to them. New paths are being suggested. Brieland & Töpfer (2020), for example, put hope in the contribution that learning machine methods might bring. However, it is important to exercise continuous monitoring, maintaining sources and methodologies.

References

Brieland, Stephanie & Töpfer, Marina (2020), *The gender pay gap revisited: Does machine learning offer new insights?*, Diskussionspapiere, No. 111, Friedrich-Alexander Universität Erlangen-Nürnberg.

Becker, Gary S. (1993) [1981], *A Treatise on the Family*, Cambridge: Harvard University Press.

Card, David; Cardoso, Ana Rute, & Kline, Patrick (2016), "Bargaining, Sorting, and the Gender Wage Gap: Quantifying the Impact of Firms on the Relative Pay of Women". *The Quarterly Journal of Economics*, 131(2), 633-686.

Cardoso, Ana Rute; Guimarães, Paulo; Portugal, Pedro & Raposo, Pedro (2016), "The sources of the gender wage gap," *Economic Bulletin and Financial Stability Report Articles and Banco de Portugal Economic Studies*. Lisboa: Banco de Portugal.

Casaca, Sara Falcão (2021), *Os Benefícios Sociais e Económicos da Igualdade Salarial entre Mulheres e Homens* (Projeto EEA-Grants 2014-2021). Available at https://genderpaygap-elimination.pt/resultados/

England, Paula & Lewin, Peter (1989), Economic and Sociological Views of Discrimination in Labor Markets: Persistence or Demise?". *Sociological Spectrum*, 9, 239 257.

Ferreira, Virgínia (2010), "A Evolução das Desigualdades entre Salários Masculinos e Femininos: Um Percurso Irregular". *In* Virgínia Ferreira (org.), *A Igualdade de Mulheres e Homens no Trabalho e no Emprego em Portugal: Políticas e Circunstâncias*. Lisboa, CITE, Cap. 4, 139-190.

Ferreira, Virgínia & Lopes, Mónica (2009), "Os Custos da Maternidade e Paternidade na Perspectiva dos Indivíduos, das Organizações e do Estado", relatório para a FCT (Projecto PIHM/SOC/63606/2005).

González, Maria do Pilar (2010), "Diferenciais salariais de género e educação em Portugal". *In* Aurora Teixeira, Sandra Silva & Pedro Teixeira (orgs.), *O que sabemos sobre a pobreza em Portugal?*. Porto: Vida Económica, Cap. 12.

Kilgour, John G. (2020), "The Gender-Based Pay Gap Is Gone." *The Journal of Total Rewards,* 29(1): 28-40.

Rubery, Jill & Grimshaw, Damian (2014), "The 40-year pursuit of equal pay: a case of constantly moving goalposts". *Cambridge Journal of Economics*, pp. 1/2 doi:10.1093/cje/beu053

IV.

**WORK, DIGITAL ECONOMY
AND THE RIGHT TO DISCONNECT**

CHAPTER 7:
DIGITAL LABOUR PLATFORMS: OPPORTUNITIES AND CHALLENGES FOR WORKERS[106]

Uma Rani[107]

Technological innovations have shaped economic landscapes, workplaces, and working time throughout history. Since the 1980s, the information and communication technology (ICT) revolution has ushered in a wave of new processes and new products and transformed some of the major sectors of the economy, such as information technology, finance and automotive industry, which in turn spurred productivity growth and stimulated economic competition (Castells, 2010). This ICT revolution also laid the foundations for the future of the internet or digital economy, e.g. by building internet infrastructure and developing digital infrastructure[108] applications (software products and services for designing). Since the early 2000s, there has been a new wave of the ICT revolution, which entails diffusion of digital innovations through the internet and digital platforms such as search engines or marketplaces, and the adoption of big data, internet of things and artificial intelligen-

---

[106] This paper was received in September 2019 and corresponds to the participation in the seminar with the same title (2nd edition of "Cátedra OIT/ILO Chair"), held at the University of Coimbra, Faculty of Economics (FEUC), on April 30, 2019.

[107] Senior Economist, Research Department, ILO, Geneva.

[108] Digital infrastructure comprises devices, servers and storage, data, and networks.

https://doi.org/10.14195/978-989-26-2277-4_13

ce. The emergence of digital labour platforms has been one of the prominent transformations in the world of work during the past decade, causing firms to outsource and conduct their business in new ways and also transforming employment practices.

In addition to providing workers with employment opportunities and access to global labour markets, digital labour platforms arguably have potential positive impacts in terms of addressing poverty and inequality in developing countries (Schriner and Oerther, 2014). The potential of these platforms to create income and employment opportunities has also attracted the attention of a lot of governments and policy makers, not only as a strategy of economic development but also as a way of addressing the growing unemployment problem in developing countries (Rani and Singh, 2019). Based on a global survey of 2,350 workers living in 75 countries, this paper looks at some of the opportunities and challenges facing workers engaged in microtask platforms and provides some policy suggestions.

1. What are digital labour platforms?

Digital labour platforms can be categorised into online web--based platforms – in which work is outsourced to a geographically dispersed crowd (microtasking), to individuals (freelancers) or to a community of developers or programmers (software or programming platforms) – and location-based platforms – which allocate work to individuals in a specific geographical area or physical locations, such as delivery workers, taxi drivers or domestic workers/cleaners (see figure 1).

This paper focuses on microtask platforms, in which workers complete short, simple and repetitive tasks that do not require any specialised training. Some of these tasks are binary and multiple choice; quality is determined based on a majority voting-based algorithm, and payment is based on the completion and approval of the task performed (Rani and Furrer, 2019). These tasks are diverse and include image identification, transcription and annotation; content moderation; data collection and processing; audio and video transcription; and translation.

Microtask platforms serve as spot labour markets that match a broad range of skills with tasks, providing a wide range of tasks or projects which can be performed by workers at a significantly lower cost and reducing transaction and start-up costs for the company, or logistic hurdles, as they can access the global pool of labour based on demand (Bourdeau and Lakhani, 2013; Bergvall-Kareborn and Howcroft, 2014). These platforms thus provide businesses and other clients with access to a large, flexible workforce (a "crowd") 24/7, so that they can complete the tasks in a short period of time. Clients use these platforms to post bulk tasks that would normally be quite expensive to perform in-house. For instance, it was estimated that it would take 1000 workers from the crowd to process data in a single day on Amazon Mechanical Turk (AMT), instead of hiring 10 workers internally for 100 days (Irani, 2015). Workers select the tasks and are paid for each individual task or piece of work completed and approved, and the platforms pay the workers the payment indicated by the client minus their fee.

Figure 1. Typology of digital labour platforms

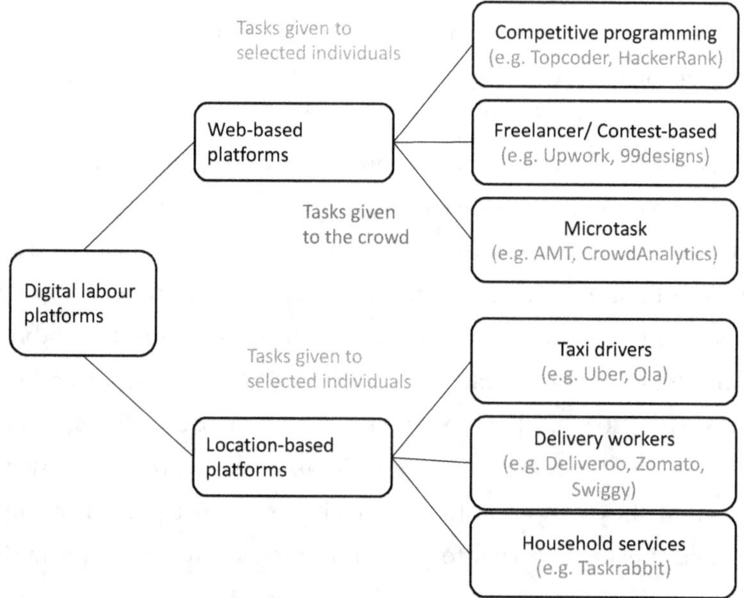

Source: Authors' elaboration

2. What are the characteristics of workers engaged in microtask platforms?

To understand who participates in microtask platforms, ILO conducted a survey in 2017 to capture the motivations of the workers and their working conditions on five major English-speaking microtask platforms.[109] These platforms include Amazon Mechanical

---

[109] As there are no global estimates of the size and composition of the workforce engaged in digital labour platforms, it is difficult to draw a representative sample of crowdworkers. So, we posted the survey as a paid task in small batches at different times of the day on these five platforms and invited workers to participate and complete the survey. There were no restrictions as to who could participate except in the case of AMT, where we targeted largely American and Indian workers to do a comparison between these two countries. At the time of the survey, according

Turk (AMT), Clickworker, CrowdFlower (rebranded as FigureEight and now taken over by Appen), Prolific (formerly Prolific Academic) and Microworkers. The working conditions captured in the survey included: work availability, work intensity, incomes and payments, rejections and non-payment, worker communication with clients and platform operators, social protection coverage and the types of work performed.

Workers from both developed[110] (64%) and developing countries[111] (36%) are engaged in these platforms (see figure 2), though their participation seems to be quite platform-specific. On AMT, a large proportion of workers come from the US, followed by India. The survey captured a sizable proportion of workers originating in the US and India on this platform, so as to make some comparisons relating to some aspects of working conditions such as pay, social protection, nature of tasks performed, and time spent on these platforms. As such, 52% of the Indian and 47% of the US workers were captured on the AMT platform. The respondents on CrowdFlower originated largely from Latin America (33%) and Europe (30%), with 13% coming from Central and Eastern Europe (CEE) and as many from North America. The majority of the survey respondents on Clickworker – a German-based platform – came

to AMT statistics, the share of American workers was around 75%, that of Indian workers was around 18%, and other countries comprised only 7%.

[110] Developed countries in this paper include Asia-Pacific (Australia, New Zealand, Singapore, Saudi Arabia, Israel and Japan), Europe (United Kingdom, Germany, Italy, Spain, Portugal, France, Croatia, the Netherlands, Austria, Greece, Belgium, Ireland, Switzerland, Finland and Sweden), Central and Eastern Europe (Romania, Poland, Bulgaria, Hungary, the Czech Republic, Lithuania, Slovakia, Estonia, Latvia, and Slovenia) and North America (the USA and Canada).

[111] For purposes of this paper, developing countries includes Asia (India, Nepal, Indonesia, Pakistan, Turkey, Bangladesh, the Philippines, Sri Lanka, Malaysia, Vietnam, Armenia, Brunei, China, Georgia, Kyrgyzstan), Africa (South Africa, Kenya, Nigeria, Morocco, Algeria, Egypt, Tunisia and Ghana), Latin America and the Caribbean (Venezuela, Brazil, Mexico, Peru, Argentina, Chile, Colombia, Ecuador, Jamaica, Bolivia and Uruguay), Central and Eastern Europe (Russia, Ukraine and Moldova) and Europe (Republic of Serbia, Bosnia and Herzegovnia, Macedonia, and Albania).

from Europe (71%) and North America (17%), and the same applied in the case of Prolific, the UK-based platform in which 53% of the respondents resided in Europe and 43% in North America. Finally, on Microworkers, the survey respondents were largely from North America (32%), followed by Asia and Pacific (30%), Europe (23%) and Africa (8%). The participation of workers from Africa was quite low in other platforms (less than 2%). Similarly, Latin American workers were largely participating in CrowdFlower, while in other platforms their participation was less than 1%, which could also be because the survey was largely based on English-speaking platforms.

Figure 2. Distribution of survey respondents across countries, crowdwork survey 2017

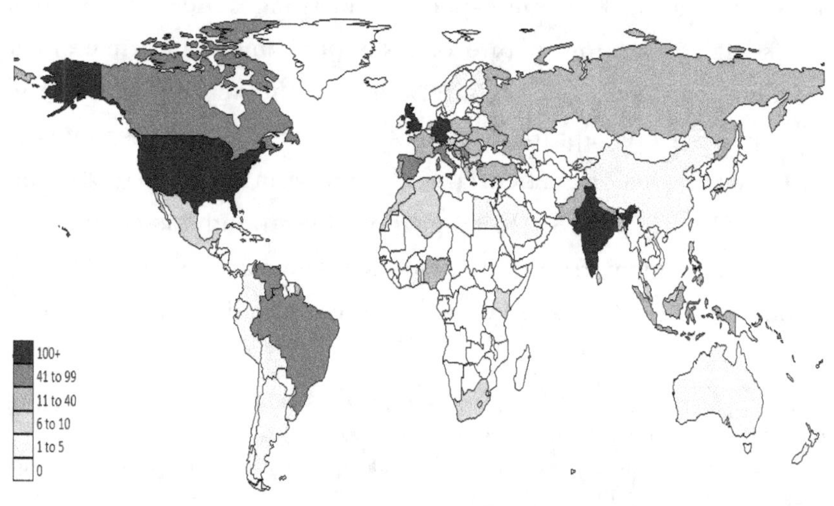

Source: ILO survey of crowdworkers, 2017

The average age of the respondents performing these tasks was 33 years globally, and it was 30 years in developing and 35 years in developed countries. In developing countries, the African and

Latin American workers were younger than their Asian counterparts. Workers across all age groups 18 to 71 years participated in microtask platforms, and a higher proportion of women than men participated in the age groups 36 to 45 years, and 46 years and above. There were gender differences, with women representing only one out of every three workers globally, and these differences were particularly skewed in developing countries, with only one out of five workers being a woman.

Globally, a very high proportion of the workers (57%) had a bachelor's degree (37%) or a postgraduate degree (20%), and a small proportion of workers had a high school diploma or less (18%), and about one-fourth had a technical certificate or some form of higher education. The education level among workers was quite high in Asia, with 80% possessing a bachelor's degree. Overall, among those with higher education (bachelor's or post graduate degree), about 57% were specialised in science and technology (12% in natural sciences and medicine, 23% in engineering and 22% in information technology) and 25% were specialised in economics, finance and accounting.

A significant proportion of survey respondents (56%) had performed tasks on microtask platforms for more than a year. Of those, about 27% had been active performing tasks on these platforms for one to two years, 19% for three to four years, and 10% had been active for more than five years. The remaining 44% of survey respondents had less than one-year's experience. About 20% of the workers from Asia had more than five year's experience and this was largely on AMT.[112]

---

[112] This is largely due to Indian workers on AMT having longer tenure. In 2012, Amazon decided to restrict new accounts to non-US workers. As a result, Indian workers faced less competition and could continue on this platform for a longer time (Berg, 2016).

Work on these microtask platforms was the main source of income for 32% of the workers, and for about half of the workers (52%) crowdwork was a secondary activity, as they were engaged in other jobs. A higher proportion of workers in developing countries (41%) had crowdwork as the main source of income compared to those in developing countries (27%). Crowdwork was a main source of income for a higher proportion of women (35%), and quite high among women in developing (46%) compared to developed countries (32%).

3. What motivates these workers to work on these platforms?

To understand the motivation of workers to participate on these platforms, we asked the survey respondents about their most important reasons for crowdworking. The most important reasons for performing crowdwork was to "complement pay from other jobs" and this reason was much more important in developed (37%) compared to developing countries (23%). The second important reason was because they "prefer to work from home", and this reason was higher in developing (24%) compared to developed countries (21%), which could also be because of distances to travel to work and traffic congestions. A significant proportion of workers in developing countries also indicated that the pay was better in these jobs (10%) compared to what was available in the offline labour market, and this was especially so in India, Brazil and Venezuela. The motivation to perform microtasks on platforms due to better pay was comparatively low in developed countries (1%).

Work on microtask platforms was also an opportunity for many workers, who, for one reason or another, could not access the offline labour market. In both developing and developed countries, about 8% of the survey respondents said that they perform tasks on these platforms because they could not find other employment opportunities. Another reason provided was that they could "only work from home", and there were strong differences by gender, with 13% of women workers globally giving this reason compared to 5% of men. These proportions were quite high among women in developing (16%) compared to developed countries (12%), due to their care responsibilities with children, the disabled and the elderly, which often prevented them from undertaking work outside their homes.

About 19% of the survey respondents indicated that they had health problems, and 54% of those also stated that their health conditions affected the type of paid work they could perform. These proportions were quite high in developed countries (24%) compared to developing countries (11%). A higher proportion of women in both developed (29%) and developing countries (15%) indicated that they had health problems, which in the case of more than half of them affected the kind of paid work they could do. For these workers, tasks on online web-based platforms such as crowdwork provided an opportunity to access work and earn an income.

4. What are the challenges faced by workers on these platforms?

While microtask platforms provide workers with opportunities to work and earn incomes, there are also a number of challenges faced by these workers. Let us take a look at some of these challenges.

Remuneration: A number of existing studies on microtask platforms mainly focusing on AMT, have found remuneration to be quite low (see e.g. Ipeirotis 2010; Berg 2016; Hara et al. 2018; Berg et al. 2018). The ILO 2017 survey collected information on the number of paid and unpaid hours to compute the hourly earnings. The findings show that on average, a worker earned US$4.43 per hour when only paid work was considered, and US$3.31 per hour when the total of paid and unpaid hours were considered. The median earnings were lower, at US$2.16 per hour when paid and unpaid work were considered. A substantial proportion of workers earn below their local minimum wages when both paid and unpaid hours of work were considered: about 64% of American workers surveyed on the AMT platform earned less than the federal minimum wage of US$7.25 per hour; only 7% of German workers surveyed on the Clickworker platform reported earnings above the German minimum wage of €8.84 per hour. Low earnings are in part also due to the substantive amounts of time spent searching for tasks, taking unpaid qualification tests, researching clients to mitigate fraud, participating in discussions on online forums, etc. On average, the ILO survey also shows workers spent 24.5 hours per week doing crowdwork, three-quarters of the time was spent doing paid work and one-quarter was spent on unpaid activities.

Workers in developing countries earned much less than their counterparts in developed countries. On average, workers in developing countries earned $2.09 per hour when total paid and unpaid work were considered, compared with developed countries where workers earned $3.94 per hour. The median earnings in developing countries was only $1.18 per hour compared to $3.02 in developed countries. Some of these differences could be explained by the nature of the tasks performed by workers in different regions and across platforms, but most of these differences also occur due to the platform design, which allows clients to choose workers from different countries, sex and age and restricts access to certain tasks to workers originating from certain countries. An analysis of US and Indian workers on AMT also revealed such differences, as many of the best-paying tasks such as content creation and editing were available only to the American workers, while low-paying tasks such as data collection, categorisation, content access, etc. were left to the Indian workers. As a result, there was a huge differential in earnings between the American and Indian workers, with the former (US$6.90 per hour) earning more than twice as much as their Indian counterparts (US$2.48 per hour) (Rani and Furrer, 2021). Such differences across regions have also been documented by other researchers (Galperin and Greppi, 2017; Beerepoot and Lambregts, 2015).

Irregularity of work: Another challenge faced by workers relates to the irregularity and insufficiency of work on these platforms. About 85% and 92% of the crowdworkers in developed and developing countries indicated that they would like to do more crowdwork. The reason for not being able to do more crowdwork was the fact that there was not enough work available, which was reported by more than half of the respondents, and enough well-paying tasks, which was reported by 17% of the respondents. The irregularity and insufficiency of work encouraged workers to search for tasks on other platforms. As a result, about 50% of the respondents reported having worked on more than one platform in the month preceding the survey, and 21% of them had worked on three or more different platforms. There was also a desire to do more work that was not crowdwork, which was expressed by 60% of respondents, while 41% reported being actively looking for paid work other than crowdwork.

Flexible work with atypical hours: While workers had the ability to set their own schedule and work from home or any other place, many workers also said that they worked long hours and atypical hours, as work was not easily available. This was especially so among workers from developing countries as they needed to adapt to the temporal distribution of jobs (Kessler, 2018; O'Neill, 2018), which limits the flexibility that these workers might otherwise enjoy. In developing countries, this often resulted in workers working for six

(21%) or seven days a week (45%), and about 69% working during the evening (6 p.m. to 10 p.m.) and 54% of the workers working during the night (10 p.m. to 5 a.m.). For many of these workers, maintaining a work-life balance was a huge challenge. The work intensity was comparatively lower among workers from developed countries, with 13% of the workers reporting working six days and 30% working seven days. Similarly, only 36% of the workers reported working during the night. Many women combined crowdwork with care responsibilities, and one out of five female workers in the sample had small children (0 to 5 years). Many women worked during the evenings and at night, and the proportion of women working during the night was higher among women from developing (46%) compared to developed countries (36%).

Deskilling and skills mismatch: Work outsourced through microtask platforms has the potential to displace/replace some forms of skilled labour with unskilled labour (Kittur et al., 2013). When tasks are disaggregated or broken down into smaller simple tasks that can be standardised, as is the case with speech transcription or the translation of a document, then it becomes possible to displace workers with non-professional crowd labour. This also has the tendency to reduce the value of skills that were earlier important in the market (Kittur et al., 2011) and these fragmented tasks have the potential to eventually be solvable by AI or machine learning (Schmidt 2017). The deskilling of work also leads to a skills mismatch, as workers who perform such tasks are often more qualified and skilled. As mentioned before, a high proportion of survey respondents performing tasks on these platforms have high levels of education. The most common tasks performed by survey respondents on microtask platforms included responding to surveys and participating in experiments (65%), accessing content on websites (46%), data collection (35%) and transcription (32%) (Berg et al., 2018). One out of five workers regularly performed content creation and editing and 8% were engaged in tasks associated with training artificial intelligence. These tasks tend to be quite repetitive and mind-numbing. And for highly educated workers with graduate-level STEM (Science, Technology, Engineering and Mathematics) education, especially from developing countries, to perform these tasks represents an underutilisation of skills and a wasted investment. Rani and Furrer (2019) use the ILO survey to show that about 44% of the highly experienced workers, i.e., those working for more than 5 years on platforms, performed content access, which reveals that tasks do not become narrower and highly specialised with experience. Workers have no choice but to perform a whole variety of tasks that are available to earn incomes.

Lack of social protection benefits: Another major challenge related to social protection coverage among the survey respondents, which was quite low, as only six out of ten respondents in 2017 were covered by health insurance and only 35% had a pension or retirement plan. In most cases this coverage came from the respondents' main job, which was not crowdwork, or consisted of job-related benefits of their family members or State-sponsored universal benefits. Workers who were mainly dependent on social protection were more likely to be unprotected. About 16% of the workers for whom crowdwork was the main source of income were covered by a retirement plan, compared with 44% of those for whom crowdwork was not the main source of income.

Lack of communication and payment: As the acceptance or approval of work was algorithmically determined through a majority voting system, this often resulted in workers' tasks being rejected and in non-payment for the work performed. This was reported by almost nine out of ten workers in the ILO survey. The majority of the survey respondents (88%) said that their rejections were not justifiable and only 12% of respondents stated that all their rejections were justifiable. Microtask platforms are set up as a one-way process in which the workers cannot communicate either with the platform or with the clients. When the tasks of the workers are unfairly rejected, they do not have the ability to appeal and this often led to frustration among workers. The rejection of work also negatively impacts the workers' rating and reputation and could lead to deactivation of their accounts. In addition, in many of these platforms, such as AMT or Microworkers, there are rejection thresholds and if the workers have a lower rating then they do not get better-paid tasks. Workers struggle to communicate with requesters and platforms, and many of them (28 to 60%, depending on the platform surveyed) have turned to worker-run online forums and social media sites either to get advice or to follow the discussions about issues facing crowdworkers. The lack of communication and the use of algorithms to evaluate the workers' tasks is quite unfair for the workers, as they do not know why their work is being rejected and are not given the opportunity to improve their performance in the future.

5. How to ensure decent work in online web-based platforms?

While many of these workers perform valuable work, there are a number of challenges that need to be addressed to ensure that workers have decent work and income security. Over the past years, there have been a number of initiatives to encourage platforms and clients to improve working conditions. For instance, the Crowdsourcing Code of Conduct, a voluntary pledge initiated by German crowdsourcing platforms established in 2017 by the German trade union, IG Metall, the German Crowdsourcing Association, and eight digital labour platforms was one of the interesting developments. The code of conduct sets out a basic set of guidelines with a view to promoting trust and fair cooperation between service providers, clients and crowdworkers. The signatory platforms established an "Ombuds Office", in cooperation with IG Metall, whose mandate is to enforce the Code of Conduct and resolve disputes between workers and signatory platforms, regardless of the location of the worker. Other initiatives have been the Turkopticon – a third-party website and browser plug-in for the Amazon Mechanical Turk (AMT) platform, which allows workers to rate clients who post tasks –, the Dynamo Guidelines for Academic Requesters on AMT, and FairCrowdWork.org.

Despite these promising efforts, the challenge of regulating globally dispersed crowdwork cannot be underestimated, as there is no government regulation of these platforms. Berg et al (2018), in their report on 'Digital labour platforms and the future of work: Towards decent work in the online world', have put forward 18 criteria with a view to ensuring decent work on digital labour platforms. The criteria include addressing employment misclassification, allowing crowdworkers to exercise their freedom of association and collective bargaining rights, ensuring transparency in payments and fees assessed by the platform, establishing strict and fair rules to govern non-payment, and establishing and enforcing clear codes of conduct for all users of the platform, among others. In addition, the report recommends three criteria for adapting social protection systems so that crowdworkers have access to social protection coverage.

The Global Commission for the Future of Work (2019) also calls on the ILO to develop an international governance system for digital labour platforms that ensures certain minimum rights and protections for workers on these platforms. It draws its inspiration from the 2006 Maritime Labour Convention, which is a labour code for seafarers that transcends geographical borders (ILO 2019a). Since the work mediated through digital platforms, especially on-line web-based work, often involves different actors based in different countries – the platform originating in one country, clients from different countries, and workers from across the globe –, it would be key to clarify the applicable legislation and institutional arrangements to ensure that workers are effectively covered in the case of cross-border arrangements. Given that the standard employment relationship remains the centrepiece of labour protection, the ILO also calls on all stakeholders "to review and where necessary clarify responsibilities and adapt the scope of laws and regulations to ensure effective protection for workers in an employment relationship. At the same time, all workers, regardless of their contractual arrangement or employment status, must equally enjoy adequate labour protection to ensure humane working conditions for everyone." (ILO, 2019: 38).

References

Beerepoot, N., B. Lambregts (2015), Competition in online job marketplaces: Towards a global labour market for outsourcing services, *Global Networks* 15(2): 236–255.

Berg, J. (2016), *Income security in the on-demand economy: findings and policy lessons from a survey of crowdworkers*. Conditions of Work and Employment Series No. 74. Geneva: ILO.

Berg, J., M. Furrer, E. Harmon, U. Rani, M.S. Silberman (2018), *Digital labour platforms and the future of work: Towards decent work in the online world*. Geneva: ILO.

Bergvall-Kareborn, B., D. Howcroft (2014), Amazon Mechanical Turk and the commodification of labour. *New Technology, Work and Employment* 29(3): 213–223.

Bourdreau, K. J., K.R. Lakhani (2013), *Using the crowd as an innovation partner.* Harvard Business Review, April 2013.

Castells, M. 2010. *The rise of the network society: The information age, Economy society and culture*. Wiley-Blackwell, UK.

Galperin, H., C. Greppi (2017), *Geographical discrimination in the gig economy.* Accessed on May 10, 2019, unpublished.

Hara, K., A. Adams, K. Milland, S. Savage, C. Callison-Burch, J.P. Bigham (2018), A data-driven analysis of workers' earnings on AMT. *Proceedings of the CHI '18 Conference*, Montreal.

International Labour Organization (ILO), (2019) *Global commission on the future of work: Working for a brighter future*, Geneva.

Ipeirotis, P.G. (2010), Analyzing the Amazon Mechanical Turk marketplace. *ACM XRDS* 17(2): 16–21.

Irani, L.C. (2015) Difference and dependence among digital workers: The case of Amazon Mechanical Turk. *South Atlantic Quarterly* 114(1): 225-234.

Kessler, S. (2018), The crazy hacks one woman used to make money on Mechanical Turk, *Wired*, 12.06.2018.

Kittur, A., J.V. Nickerson, M.S. Bernstein, E.M. Gerber, A. Shaw, J. Zimmerman, M. Lease, J.J. Horton (2013), The future of crowd work. *Proceedings of the CSCW '13 Conference*, San Antonio, TX, pp. 1301-1318.

O'Neill, J. (2018), From crowdwork to Ola Auto: Can platform economies improve livelihoods in emerging markets? Pp. 28–31 in: H. Galperin, A. Alarcon (eds.), *The future of work in the Global South*. Ottawa, ON: International Development Research Centre.

Rani, U., M. Furrer (2021) Digital labour platforms and new forms of flexible work in developing countries: Algorithmic management of work and workers. *Competition and Change* 25 (2): 212-236, DOI: 10.1177/1024529420905187

Rani, U., M. Furrer (2019) On-demand digital economy: Can experience ensure work and income security for microtask workers?, *Journal of Economics and Statistics*, 239 (3): 565–97.

Rani, U., P. J. Singh (2019) Digital platforms, data, and development: Implications for workers in developing economies, *Comparative Labour Law and Policy Journal*.

Schmidt, F. A. (2017), *Digital labour markets in the platform economy: Mapping the political challenges of crowd work and gig work*. Bonn: Friedrich-Ebert-Stiftung.

Schriner, A., D. Oerther (2014), No really, (crowd) work is the silver bullet. *Procedia Engineering* 78: 224–228.

COMMENT:
A BRIEF NOTE ON LABOUR PLATFORMS AND WORKERS' DIGNITY

Elísio Estanque[113] and Dora Fonseca[114]

The study presented in chapter 7 (Uma Rani) addresses a topic of great importance – the problem of the digitalisation of work and the resulting effects on society. The author stresses not only the "transformative" role of digitalisation but also its paradoxical nature, which manifests itself at several levels. Such trends as digitalisation and digital labour platforms, which enable instant connectivity between service providers (supply) and end users in exchange for payment, are viewed either as being disruptive (because they raise the spectre of the end of work) or as promising paths to autonomy and self-fulfilment. Using a comparative perspective, Rani's text provides empirical data about a reality that is both complex and, given its inherent characteristics, difficult to measure. All over the world, digital labour platforms have become increasingly prominent in everyday life. Due to the restrictions imposed by the COVID-19 pandemic, they have grown in importance in recent times. Furthermore, their meanings vary, depending on the contexts in which this platform-based type of work takes place.

---

[113] University of Coimbra, Faculty of Economics, Centre for Social Studies.

[114] University of Coimbra, Centre for Social Studies and CoLABOR - Collaborative Laboratory for Labour, Employment and Social Protection.

https://doi.org/10.14195/978-989-26-2277-4_14

Digitalisation poses a challenge to traditional forms of capital and labour allocation in capitalist systems and heralds the end of the employment relationship (Campos Lima, 2020; Degryse, 2016; Vandaele, 2018; Srnicek, 2017). Platform companies share a business model based on costs that go down as supply goes up. The financial capacity of these companies is ensured, among other things, by the availability of a redundant workforce, and thus becomes especially attractive to financial capital markets (Langley & Leyshon, 2016; Srnicek, 2017). Platforms are a "distinct mode of socio-technical intermediation" of business and contractual stipulations that are incorporated into broader processes of capitalisation and value extraction (Campos Lima & Perista, 2020).

The text highlights the heterogeneity of digital platforms. This diversity is variously reflected in multiple instances, through which the diversity of the offer (the service providers) is also multiplied. One of the innovative aspects of the study lies in the fact that the empirical data points to significant differences in the characteristics of platform-based work in central and peripheral countries. Although those differences are also mentioned in other works, here they get to be clearly shown and empirically substantiated. While the author does an important job in terms of characterising supply from a comparative perspective, she says nothing about collective action and regulation, two areas that have been covered by other authors and in which important, albeit slow, progress has been made. A more explicit mention of such studies would have been useful to give a fuller picture of the current situation.

The platformisation of work can be definded as a way of mobilising labour based on digital platforms specifically designed to allow instant connectivity between service providers and end users in exchange for payment (Favereau, 2016). The hierarchical structure of digital platforms (Daugareilh et al., 2019; EIF, 2019; ILO, 2018; Rodrigues et al., 2016) favours a capital-labour relationship in which the commanding, procedural and disciplinary powers of the former are algorithmised and unilaterally exercised over the latter (EIF, 2019). Benefiting from a misclassification of their economic activities and legal status (Huws, 2020; Rogers, 2016; Leal Amado & Moreira, 2019), platforms such as Uber force subcontracted workers to invest in supplying and maintaining the means of production, further exposing them to the extraction of (financialised, e.g. *via* loan and insurance products) value. Such exposure is conducive to labour precariousness.

With respect to governance, the benefits resulting from the hierarchical structure of the platforms are not so obvious (Rogers, 2016; Leal Amado & Moreira, 2019; Dufresne & Leterme, 2021; ILO, 2018). Substituting human oversight and disciplinary power with algorithmic coordination raises new questions regarding transparency and accountability in management practices and adds complexity (both at the theoretical and legal level) to any attempt to resolve the problem of indeterminacy caused by the fact that the work re-lationship has become digitally mediated (ILO, 2018; Leal Amado & Moreira, 2019; Almeida et al., 2020). In addition, digital platforms take advantage of existing gaps and ambiguities in domestic and international regulations and put to use their mediating nature to transfer market risks to workers and expose them to global com-petition, thereby expanding the gray areas occupied by workers in terms of social protection rights, bargaining power, and collective action (Huws, 2020; Almeida et al., 2020; Daugareilh et al., 2019; Drahokoupil & Piasna, 2019; Dufresne & Leterme, 2021).

However, the very "indeterminacy" that characterises this form of work (the employment relationship) and the repercussions of that indeterminacy are giving rise to the creation and reinvention of collective structures of worker mobilisation and representation – including lawsuits – aimed at holding employers accountable and ensuring labour rights and protections (Dufresne & Leterme, 2021;

Rogers, 2016). These strategies are mutually reinforcing and pose important challenges. Worker organisation and action need to be defined at multiple geographic and regulatory levels (Campos Lima & Perista, 2020; Dufresne & Leterme, 2021). At present, they range from worker strikes and direct action to trade union action, thus encompassing the local, national and transnational level.

The fragmentation of working communities, the disregard for working time regulations and the diversity of workers' sociological profiles are proving a challenge both for emerging collectives and for established trade unions (Benassi & Vlandas, 2016; Fonseca, 2020; Lenaerts et al., 2017; Vandaele, 2018; Campos Lima et al., 2021). In these circumstances, the mobilisation of platform workers leads (or can lead) to union renewal, as it involves the mobilisation of multiple power resources (Estanque et al., 2020; Lévesque & Murray, 2010; Langley, 2008). In this way, trade unions are encouraged to rethink their own role and strategies of representation, which can go from joining existing structures to finding alternatives to them. But the struggle of platform workers and platform workers' collectives has also been waged in the labour courts and through the legislative process. As far as legislation is concerned, correct classification of the relationship between platform-based companies and their workers is the new focus of action. Recent court decisions have ratified the subordinate nature of the relationship between workers and platform-based companies and are fueling disagreement over regulations on the status of platform workers.

Most neoliberal governments have fostered solutions that subject labour law to the principles of uberisation (the digital self-employed in the US; "third status" workers in Europe), the exception being the Spanish model of unconditional employment. In the context of the European Union, a directive on platform workers is currently under discussion and there is a possibility that it will benefit from national alternatives that go against the grain. New measures to assess the impact of international developments in this area are also under way, notably in Portugal, where a new legal framework is expected in the near future. The as yet incipient participation of platform workers in collective bargaining oscillates between sectoral and company-level negotiation, depending on the labour relations system of each country. Among the challenges with which they are faced is the need to consider platform-based companies as political subjects that are party to the employment relationship. In this regard, the types of approach obtaining in the Nordic countries point to alternative paths requiring a critical assessment that may make it possible to account for institutional diversity and thus allow us to adequately address the need to provide digital platform workers with dignified working conditions.

References

Benassi, C., T. Vlandas (2016), "Union inclusiveness and temporary agency workers: The role of power resources and union ideology", *European Journal of Industrial Relations*, Vol.22(1), 5-22.

Campos Lima, M. and H. Perista (2020), New Employment Forms and Challenges to Industrial Relations: Country Report Portugal (NEWEFIN). https://aiashsi.uva.nl/en/projects-a-z/newefin/drafts-country-reports/newefin-drafts-countryreports.html (accessed on March 9, 2022).

Campos Lima M da P, Martins D, Costa AC, Velez A. (2021), "Internal devaluation and economic inequality in Portugal: challenges to industrial relations in times of crisis and recovery", *Transfer: European Review of Labour and Research*. doi:10.1177/1024258921995006

Daugareilh I., C. Degryse and P. Pochet (eds.) (2019), *The platform economy and social law: Key issues in comparative perspective*, Brussels: ETUI.

Degryse C., (2016), *Digitalisation of the economy and its impact on labor markets*, Brussels: ETUI.

Drahokoupil, J. and A. Piasna (2019), *Work in the platform economy: Deliveroo riders in Belgium and the Smart arrangement*, Brussels: ETUI.

Dufresne, A., C. Leterme (2021), *App Workers United. The struggle for rights in the gig economy*, Brussels: GUE/NGL European Parliament.

EIF [European Investment Fund] (2019), European Small Business Finance Outlook December 2019, EIF Research & Market Analysis, Working Paper 2020/61. Available at: https://www.eif.org/news_centre/publications/EIF_Working_Paper_2019_61.htm_

Estanque, Elísio; Costa, Hermes Augusto; Fonseca, Dora; Silva, Manuel Carvalho da (2020) *Trade union powers. Implosion or reinvention?* Newcastle upon Tyne, Cambridge Scholars Publishing.

Favereau, O. (2016), The impact of financialisation of the economy on enterprises and more specifically on labour relations, International Labour Organization. Available at: https://www.researchgate.net/publication/310801437_The_impact_of_financialisation_of_the_economy_on_enterprises_and_more_specifically_on_labour_relations (accessed on March 9, 2022).

Fonseca, D. (2020), "Collective action at a crossroad: Trade unions and social movements in the age of labour austerity", *in* Carmo, R., J. Simões (eds) *Protest, youth and precariousness: the unfinished fight against austerity in Portugal.* New York: Berghahn Books, 72-91.

ILO [International Labour Organization] (2018) *Digital labour platforms and the future of work: Towards decent work in the online world*, Geneva: International Labour Office.

Langley, P. (2008), *The everyday life of global finance: saving and borrowing in America*, Oxford: Oxford University Press.

Langley, P. and A. Leyshon (2016), Platform capitalism: the intermediation and capitalisation of digital circulation, *Finance and Society*, Vol.2 (1), 1-14.

Lenaerts, K., M. Beblavý, and Z. Kilhoffer (2017), *Government responses to the platform economy: Where do we stand?*, Brussels: CEPS.

Lévesque, C., and G. Murray (2010), "Understanding union power: resources and capabilities for renewing union capacity", *Transfer: European Review of Labour and Research*, Vol. 16(3), 333–350.

Rogers, B. (2016), Employment rights in the platform economy: Getting back to basics, *Harvard Law & Policy Review*, Vol.10, pp. 479-520. Available at: http://dx.doi.org/10.2139/ssrn.2641305 (accessed on March 9, 2022).

Rodrigues, J., A. C. Santos and N. Teles (2016), *A financeirização do Capitalismo em Portugal*, Lisboa: Actual.

Srnicek, N. (2017), *Platform capitalism*, Cambridge: Polity.

Vandaele, K. (2018), "Will trade unions survive in the platform economy? Emerging patterns of platform workers' collective voice and representation in Europe", *Working Paper 2018.05*. Brussels: ETUI.

CHAPTER 8:
WORKING ANYTIME, ANYWHERE:
THE EVOLUTION OF TELEWORK AND ITS EFFECTS ON THE WORLD OF WORK[115]

Jon C. Messenger[116]

1. Introduction

New Information and Communications Technologies (New ICTs), such as smartphones and tablet computers, have revolutionised everyday work and life in the 21st century. On the one hand, they enable constant connection with friends and family, as well as with work colleagues and supervisors; on the other hand, paid work may increasingly intrude into the time periods and physical spaces normally reserved for personal life. Crucial to this development is the detachment of work from traditional office spaces. 21st-century office work is often supported by internet connections, and thus can be done from basically anywhere and at any time. This new

---

[115] This paper was received in February 2020 and corresponds to the author's participation in the seminar "Right to disconnect" (2nd edition of "Cátedra OIT/ILO Chair"), held at the University of Coimbra, Faculty of Economics (FEUC), on April 30, 2019. A quite similar version of this text was previously published in *IUSLabor* 3/2017, ISSN 1699-2938, pp. 301-312.

[116] Team Leader, Working Conditions Group, WORKQUALITY Department, ILO Geneva.

https://doi.org/10.14195/978-989-26-2277-4_15

independence of work from place changes the role of technology in the work environment dramatically. Scholars are increasingly concerned with the advantages and disadvantages of New ICTs for working time, workplace relations, individual and organisational performance, occupational safety and health, and work-life balance.

A close analysis of the relevant literature reveals that research on the detachment of work from the employer's premises and its effects actually dates back to the previous century (Messenger and Gschwind, 2015). In the 1970s and 1980s, visionaries such as Jack Nilles (Nilles, 1975, 1988) and Allan Toffler (Toffler, 1980) predicted that the work of the future would be relocated into, or close to, employees' homes with the help of modern technology – so-called "Telecommuting" or "Telework". To fully understand the effects of New ICTs on the world of work, it is thus important to make a conceptual link between the early days of Telework/Telecommuting and such arrangements today. Technological advances are the motor of change in this context, and they have fostered *the evolution of Telework in three distinct stages or "generations"* (see Messenger and Gschwind, 2016 for a full discussion of this evolutionary process). First, personal computers and fixed telephones replaced long commuting hours between home and the office; this was the First Generation of Telework, the Home Office. Next, laptop computers and mobile phones enabled wireless, portable work "on the move" from locations other than home or the office (so-called "third spaces"), accompanied by a fast-growing dispersion of the Internet and the World Wide Web; this was the beginning of mobile working, the Mobile Office, which is the Second Generation of Telework. Finally, online connections via radio links and the shrinking of transistors triggered the development of New ICTs (e.g., smartphones, tablet computers). *New ICTs enabled the mobile, virtual connection of workers to the "office" from almost anywhere at any time*; this is the Third Generation of Telework, the Virtual Office (Messenger and

Gschwind, 2016). Analysing the advancements of technology and how they shaped the evolution of telework over these three generations from the 1970s up to the present time sheds a new light on the term, "telework". Today's location-independent, technology-enabled new ways of working, from the mobile full-time sales person to the occasional work-related e-mail or phone call from home, are all part of the same (r)evolution in the inter-relationship between paid work and personal life.

This paper considers the effects of this "Third Generation Telework" – which the joint ILO-Eurofound report refers to as Telework/ICT-Mobile Work (T/ICTM) – on the world of work. T/ICTM work can be defined as the use of ICTs – such as smartphones, tablets, laptops and desktop computers – for the purposes of work outside the employer's premises. The paper synthesises research from that joint report, which was carried out by the European Foundation for the Improvement of Living and Working Conditions (Eurofound) network of European correspondents in 10 EU Member States – Belgium, Finland, France, Germany, Hungary, Italy, the Netherlands, Spain, Sweden and the UK – and by ILO country experts in five countries from other regions of the world – Argentina, Brazil, India, Japan and the US. These national contributors were asked to review and summarise the findings from the available datasets and research literature on the subject of T/ICTM in their respective countries.

In addition, the paper classifies employees performing T/ICTM work in relation to their place of work (home, office and/or another location) and also the intensity and frequency of their work using ICTs outside the employer's premises. The following groups of T/ICTM workers were identified: regular home-based teleworkers; occasional T/ICTM workers, with mid-to-low mobility and frequency of work outside the employer's premises, either at home or another location; and high mobile T/ICTM workers, who have a high frequency of working in various places outside the employer's premises, including working from home.

The extent of the adoption of T/ICTM work across different countries, and its effects on working time, performance, work-life balance, and health and well-being are analysed using information from the 15 national studies, supplemented by data from the sixth European Working Conditions Survey (EWCS, 2015). These research findings can contribute to the development of effective policies in the areas of digitalisation, fair working conditions and decent work in Europe and other regions of the world.

2. Incidence and Intensity of Telework and ICT-Mobile Work

The incidence of T/ICTM work seems to be related to the level of technological development in various countries, but the actual adoption of such work arrangements is also closely linked to economic structures and cultures of work. Countries analysed in this study with relatively high shares of workers using ICTs to perform work outside the employer's premises are Finland, Japan, the Netherlands, Sweden and the US. Different forms of T/ICTM work can be expected to continue to develop on different paths. While working regularly with ICTs from outside the employer's premises is still comparatively rare in most of the countries analysed, the findings of this study suggest that important changes are taking place for a growing part of the workforce; the number of employees working flexibly in relation to space and time is growing – and will likely continue to grow – enabled by ICT developments. However, T/ICTM work will probably not grow across all occupations and in all sectors. Rather, it is more likely to become an established work arrangement for those whose tasks are already ICT-enabled.

However, current trends suggest that larger shares of workers will have ICT-enabled jobs in the future (EWCS, 2015).

The incidence of T/ICTM work varies substantially across countries, ranging from 2% to 40% of all employees, depending on the particular country and the frequency with which employees carry out T/ICTM work. Across the EU, it has been estimated that at least a total of about 17% of employees do T/ICTM work (EWCS, 2015). When occasional T/ICTM work is included, such as phone calls or emails outside the office, the figure rises to an estimated 40% of all employees in Japan and the US.

There are important differences in the incidence of T/ICTM work for different groups of workers. T/ICTM work is more common among professionals and managers, but is also relevant for clerical support and sales workers. Regarding gender, in general men are more likely to perform T/ICTM work than women in all of the countries analysed in this study. However, women tend to use more regular home-based telework (rather than working in other places outside the office) and in most contexts they appear to do so mainly to balance work and family-related tasks. This suggests that gender matters in relation to T/ICTM work, and that country-specific gender roles and models of work and family life are likely shaping the use of ICTs for work outside the employer's premises.

3. The Effects of Telework and ICT-Mobile Work

The results presented in this paper demonstrate that the working hours of T/ICTM workers, and particularly high mobile T/ICTM workers, are typically longer than of those workers who always work at the employer's premises. T/ICTM workers in general are also more likely to perform paid work in the evenings and on weekends than those workers who always work in the office, although they are less likely to work at night. Finally, a substantially higher share of T/ICTM workers enjoy a significant degree of working time autonomy than their office-based counterparts, which is important in relation to the reported work-life balance of workers. The findings also show differences among countries, which seem to be related to country-specific working time patterns, cultures and gender roles. How workers experience their working time qualitatively and the implications of these new time patterns for working time regulation need to be further explored.

The studies referred to in the national reports indicate generally positive effects of T/ICTM work on individual performance. The potential for an increase in productivity with T/ICTM work is mainly related to the space and time flexibility that such work offers and the associated consequences, such as reduced commuting time, savings on office space, increased working time autonomy, innovative work behaviour, as well as the possibility of working longer and with fewer interruptions. Individual characteristics like motivation and skills seem to play a role, but so, too, does work efficiency associated with the use of ICTs. Other issues of relevance include the use of teleworking for maintaining business continuity in the case of natural disasters or other crises, and companies addressing mobility issues among employees.

Regarding the effects of T/ICTM work on work-life balance, it can be concluded that T/ICTM work, particularly working from home (home-based telework), appears to have a positive effect on overall work-life balance, mainly because of the reduction in commuting time and increased autonomy to organise working time based on individual workers' needs and preferences. At the same time, there is some risk of overlap between work and private or family life – that is, work-home interference – because of longer hours of work and the combination of paid work and other responsibilities, which may result in increased work-family conflict.

Although it appears that T/ICTM work can help to facilitate a better work-life balance for workers, it seems that a significant part of this work arrangement has a supplemental character – that is, it leads to working beyond normal/contractual working hours, which often appears to be unpaid. Therefore, this arrangement does not always reduce work-family conflict. On the contrary, the findings of this study show that a high level of use of ICTs outside the employer's premises can jeopardise work-life balance. In fact, in all types of T/ICTM work there is a clear risk of working time impinging on non-working time. This is a consequence of the typically longer working days and weeks of employees doing T/ICTM work, but seems also to be related to a lack of 'boundary management'. Thus, it seems that the higher working time autonomy of employees doing T/ICTM can only contribute to improved work-life balance for regular home-based teleworkers and those working only occasionally outside the employer's premises; it does not seem to have this effect for those doing high mobile T/ICTM or T/ICTM work with high intensity.

There are also important differences in these effects according to gender: Women tend to work shorter hours in T/ICTM work, and female workers seem to get slightly better work-life balance results than men when they do T/ICTM work. In this regard, women tend to use more regular home-based telework (rather than working in other places outside 'the office'), and in most contexts they appear to do so mainly to balance work and family-related tasks. In addition, it is worth noting that managers generally have different motives for performing T/ICTM work themselves, and they are more likely to encounter difficulties regarding work-life balance.

Employees doing T/ICTM work also seem to be exposed to risks to their health and well-being. While a higher share of workers among those doing T/ICTM work report a positive effect of this type of work on their health than other workers, there is also conversely a higher percentage of workers reporting a negative effect of such work on their health. Apart from specific job characteristics in the various occupations, the health and well-being risks faced by these employees are associated with ergonomic issues that arise while they are working outside the employer's premises. More importantly, T/ICTM work, particularly high mobile T/ICTM work, is associated with psychosocial risk factors related to work intensity, supplemental hours of work and longer working hours overall, which appear to have a negative impact on stress, sleeping problems and the perceived impact of work on health. Autonomy and support from colleagues can play a role in moderating these effects, but the findings suggest that these factors alone will not fully prevent some of the negative consequences. Reducing the intensity of work for the high mobile employees and reducing the supplemental hours for home-based teleworkers could potentially have a greater impact.

All of these findings suggest that the effects of T/ICTM work are highly ambiguous and perhaps even contradictory. Specifically, it appears that T/ICTM work is not unequivocally advantageous compared to traditional office work at the employer's premises. Neither does this type of work arrangement seem to result in mainly negative effects. On the positive side, T/ICTM workers report a reduction in commuting time, greater autonomy regarding the organisation of their working time, better overall work-life balance and higher productivity. The disadvantages of T/ICTM work with which workers seem to struggle the most are its tendency to extend working hours, create an overlap between paid work and personal life due to a blurring of work-life boundaries, and also lead to the intensification of work. It appears that many of these ambiguous or paradoxical effects have to do with the interactions among ICT use, the place of work in specific work environments and the characteristics of different occupations. Moreover, whether T/ICTM work substitutes for work in the office, or instead supplements it, appears to be an important factor affecting whether the reported outcomes are positive or negative.

4. Policy Suggestions

It is necessary to go beyond a focus on whether T/ICTM work arrangements are 'good' or 'bad': clearly, they can be either or even both at the same time. Rather, given the highly ambiguous effects of T/ICTM work, we need to understand under what specific conditions both employees and employers can benefit from such work arrangements. In this regard, this section tries to shed some light on this topic for policymakers, social partners, scholars and all those interested in the future of work, in order to understand the technology-driven changes that are occurring, and help shape such changes in a way that can benefit societies, while addressing the potentially negative side-effects. In light of this objective, this section presents some policy suggestions designed to promote such beneficial T/ICTM work.

Because the use of ICTs outside the employer's premises, overall, brings benefits for both employees and companies, policymakers – including governments and social partners – should try to address the issue in such a way that the positive effects are accentuated and the negative effects are diminished. For example, this could be done by promoting 'partial' (part-time) T/ICTM work and occasional T/ICTM work, while restricting informal, supplemental T/ICTM work, excessively long working hours, and high levels of mobility and work intensity. In terms of the latter, a more rational use of ICTs is necessary, as is the creation of conditions that make that possible.

In practical terms, the organisation of working time is changing and working time regulation needs to take this reality into account.

Working time and non-working time have to be treated differently according to the type of T/ICTM work that employees are doing. Regulations have to be clear in this respect. In this context, it is particularly important to address the issue of supplemental T/ICTM work, which may well be unpaid overtime. Moreover, it is necessary to consider how the organisation of working time is changing in connection with ICT developments and, more broadly, what that means for limitations on working hours and particularly for the need to ensure that minimum rest periods are respected.

A major challenge of T/ICTM work for the application of OSH prevention principles and of workers' health and safety legislation is related to the difficulties faced by employers regarding the supervision of the working environment and the working conditions of their employees' place of work when it is outside the employer's premises. EU-OSHA's project 'Foresight on new and emerging risks in occupational safety and health associated with ICT and work location by 2025' will produce scenarios that will help policymakers exploring strategic and policy options to address the challenges to workers' safety and health associated with T/ICTM work (EU-OSHA, 2016).

In order to fully harness the potential of T/ICTM work and improve the working conditions of employees performing such work, there is a need for training for both the employees affected and their managers on the effective use of ICTs when working remotely, the potential risks, and how to effectively manage the flexibility that this work arrangement provides. The blurring of boundaries is not necessarily negative if it is well managed. In relation to this aspect, it is important to work on building trust between employees and managers and to consider that those negative effects could be effectively cushioned with more appropriate managerial guidance. In this context, it appears that a higher degree of employee autonomy can enhance both work-life balance and individual performance.

In the context of policies aimed at increasing participation in the labour market of certain groups, including older workers, women with young children and people with disabilities, T/ICTM work can play a relevant role, especially in the context of an ageing population. Examples from some countries show that T/ICTM forms a part of policies for promoting social inclusion and increasing participation in the labour market.

The social partners are generally well positioned to address the topic of T/ICTM work, particularly in a number of EU countries, and especially in those companies where employee representation exists. Governmental initiatives and national or sectoral collective agreements are important for providing the overall framework for T/ICTM work arrangements. Of course, in the end practical application of T/ICTM will take place at company/organisational level, and thus it is also important to take into account the variety of contexts, which depend on the type of job and how ICTs are being used.

Policies regarding T/ICTM work at the national, sectoral and organisational levels need to be adapted dynamically to technological advancements, as well as the needs and preferences of workers and employers. Therefore, it is important that these frameworks provide sufficient space to develop company-specific T/ICTM work arrangements that meet both workers' and employers' needs and preferences. For example, the European Framework Agreement on Telework could be adapted to take account of the non-regular, informal aspect of teleworking and the mobile aspect of the phenomenon.

Finally, the findings of this study regarding differences in the conditions of work associated with different types of T/ICTM work, for example between home-based telework and high mobile T/ICTM work, have to be considered. Measures should tackle the specific reasons underlying negative effects on working conditions identified by the study. For example, to protect workers' health, measures are needed to restrict informal, supplemental T/ICTM work by limiting the availability for work during those times typically reserved for personal life and rest periods.

5. Conclusion

New ICTs, such as smartphones and tablet computers, have revolutionised everyday work and life in the 21st century. On the one hand, they enable us to constantly connect with friends and family as well as with work colleagues and supervisors; on the other hand, paid work becomes increasingly intrusive into the times and spaces normally reserved for personal life. Crucial to this development is the detachment of work from traditional office spaces. Today's office work is largely supported by Internet connections, and can thus be done at any time and from almost anywhere. This new spatial independence changes the role of technology in the work environment dramatically, offering both new opportunities and new challenges.

The future expansion of T/ICTM work is likely to manifest itself as a long series of tremors rather than as a sudden earthquake. Ultimately, however, it will lead to potentially profound consequences for working and living conditions. The policy suggestions presented above point to the importance of informing all parties – workers, employers and public authorities – about the advantages and disadvantages of different forms of T/ICTM work, and how to implement such work arrangements effectively. More research is needed on the subject, as well as a closer cooperation between policymakers, employers, workers and scholars, to pave the way for an adaptation of T/ICTM work to the rapidly changing world of work in the 21st century.

References

Full reference details for each of the national studies used in the joint ILO-Eurofound report are provided below.

Argentina:
Boiarov, S. (2015), T/ICTM and its effects in Argentina (unpublished ILO report).

Belgium:
Vermandere, C. (2015), T/ICTM and its effects in Belgium (unpublished Eurofound contribution).

Brazil:
Mello, A. (2015), T/ICTM and its effects in Brazil (unpublished ILO report).

Finland:
Lönnroos, L. T.; Tuomivaara, S. (Oxford Research AB and Finnish Institute of Occupational Health) (2015), T/ICTM and its effects in Finland (unpublished Eurofound contribution).

France:
Schulze-Marmeling; S., Turlan, F. (IR Share) (2015), T/ICTM and its effects in France (unpublished Eurofound contribution).

Germany:
Vogel, S. (2015), T/ICTM and its effects in Germany (unpublished Eurofound contribution).

Hungary:
Belyo, P. T/ICTM and its effects in Hungary (unpublished Eurofound contribution)

India:
Noronha, E.; D'Cruz, P. (IIM Ahmedabad) (2015), T/ICTM and its effects in India (unpublished ILO report).

Italy:
Fondazione Giacomo Brodolini Moncini (2015), T/ICTM and its effects in Italy (unpublished Eurofound contribution).

Japan:
Sato, A. (2015), T/ICTM and its effects in Japan (unpublished ILO report).

Netherlands:
Kraan, K.; Houtman, I. (TNO) (2015), T/ICTM and its effects in the Netherlands (unpublished Eurofound contribution).

Spain:

Duran, J. and IKEI (2015), T/ICTM and its effects in Spain (unpublished Eurofound contribution).

Sweden:

Gustafsson, A.-K; Johanson, E. (Oxford Research), T/ICTM and its effects in Spain (unpublished Eurofound contribution).

United Kingdom:

Adam, D. (2015), T/ICTM and its effects in the UK (unpublished Eurofound contribution).

United States:

Lister, K.; Harnish, T. (Global Workplace Analytics) (2015), T/ICTM and its effects in the US (unpublished ILO report).

Other References:

EU-OSHA (2016), *Foresight of new and emerging occupational safety and health risks associated with information and communications technologies and work locations by 2025*, web page, accessed 1 February 2017.

Eurofound (2010), *Telework in the European Union*, Publications Office of the European Union, Luxembourg.

Eurofound (2012), *Organisation of working time: Implications for productivity and working conditions*, Publications Office of the European Union, Luxembourg.

Eurofound, *Sixth European Working Conditions Survey (2015)*, web page, accessed 1 February 2017.

Eurofound (2015), *New forms of employment*, Publications Office of the European Union, Luxembourg.

Eurofound (2016), *Sixth European Working Conditions Survey 2015: Overview report*, Publications Office of the European Union, Luxembourg.

Messenger, J.; Gschwind, L. (2015), *Telework, New ICTs and their effects on working time and work-life balance: Review of the literature* (unpublished), ILO, Geneva.

Messenger, J.; Gschwind, L. (2016), 'Three generations of telework: New ICTs and the (r)evolution from home office to virtual office', *New Technology, Work and Employment*, Vol. 31, No. 3, pp. 195-208.

Nilles, J.M. (1975), Telecommunications and Organizational Decentralization, *IEEE Transactions on Communications*, 23, 10, 1142-1147.

Nilles, J.M. (1988), Traffic reduction by telecommuting: A status review and selected bibliography, *Transportation Research Part A: General*, 22, 4, 301-317.

Toffler, A. (1980), *The Third Wave* (New York: Bantam).

COMMENT:

WORKING EVERYWHERE, ALL THE TIME? TELEWORK AND THE RIGHT TO DISCONNECT

Catarina Frade[117] and Tiago Santos Pereira[118]

1. Telework as a symptom of changes in the world of work

"Today I am taking work home!" Once, these words signalled an exceptional, and short-lived, period of greater pressure at work that led to a crossing of the boundaries between the workplace and home. At those times, when working hours were insufficient to carry out the scheduled, or extraordinary, tasks, family home was a last resort to take care of pending work. This practice and discourse were typically only available to the more qualified workers, mostly in the service sector, who had greater responsibility within an organisation, and who could manage their working time and space. In addition, the sporadic incidence of these practices was a matter of delicate negotiation within the family. The management of the boundaries between office and home, in all its particularity, was then used in film scripts, that precisely explored the latent ambiguities between couples on account of the long days of work in the office or the recurring days of work at home.

---

[117] University of Coimbra, Faculty of Economics, Centre for Social Studies.

[118] University of Coimbra, Centre for Social Studies and CoLABOR - Collaborative Laboratory for Labour, Employment and Social Protection.

https://doi.org/10.14195/978-989-26-2277-4_16

Jon Messenger's analysis, in *Working anytime, anywhere: The evolution of telework and its effects on the world of work*, presents the contemporary counterpoint of the breaking of those boundaries between home and office that teleworking has intensified and of which it is the most obvious example. In the world of telework, we do not take home some work, some of the time. We simply work from home, without necessarily questioning the ways in which the boundaries between work space and family space, between working time and personal time, between professional life and personal and family life, have increasingly become invisible. If, previously, the occasional nature of remote working, which essentially represented an expansion of working hours and not a switch between workspaces, could be a source of ambiguities, now, in this present of telework, those ambiguities are permanently latent and inherent in the employment relationship. Any reflection on the emergence of telework and its effects on the world of work cannot avoid these tensions.

The COVID-19 pandemic has given telework a visibility and centrality in society that it previously lacked, but Jon Messenger, writing before the explosion of telework during the pandemic, reminds us that the use of telework is the result of a process that has been ongoing for several decades. The information and communication technologies (ICT), which form the technological infrastructure network – foreseen by technofuturists such as Alvin Toffler decades ago – on which distance communication is based, are central to the current possibility of teleworking, but are also the platform on which our personal and professional lives converge, blurring the boundaries that separate them. When computers, once large machines that could occupy entire rooms that were used only by experts, became the PC – the small personal computer "everyone" could use –, a huge step was taken in the process that facilitates teleworking. We certainly value these advances. We are unable to think about current life – which Messenger characterises as a third phase of teleworking – without recourse to the services provided by the personal computer, the tablet or the smartphone, without the internet, email or search engines. However, as Jon Messenger points out, our dependence on technology and the ease with which we communicate at a distance comes at the cost of diluting personal and professional spaces, particularly in the experience of teleworking.

2. The reproduction of inequalities through telework

On the basis of studies carried out by the Eurofound, Jon Messenger notes that, on the international level, there is wide variation in the use of telework, reflecting different levels of technological development, as well as economic structures and work cultures. From the outset, teleworking assumes a predominant culture of trust in the workplace that allows teleworkers greater degrees of autonomy. Given this, it is not surprising that, in Europe, the Nordic countries, traditionally societies with the highest levels of trust, show a higher incidence of teleworking. In Portugal, a recent study developed by the Collaborative Laboratory for Labour, Employment and Social Protection (CoLABOR) and coordinated by one of the current authors (Pereira et al., 2021), established that only 6% of employees had had a non-occasional experience of teleworking prior to the pandemic. This value is much lower than that of some European countries, but it exploded during the pandemic. It reached 35% during the first confinement (March-April 2020), when teleworking was mandatory wherever it was functionally possible, and continued as a regular practice for more than 20% of workers in Portugal during the remainder of 2020.

However, the ability to carry out work remotely, with the support of ICT, depends on the specific functions of each worker, conditions largely determined by the worker's specific sector of activity. Messenger alludes to this, but the study cited above (Pereira et al., 2021) clearly identifies significant inequalities in access to telework, noticeably in the periods of mandatory confinement during the pandemic. There is a clear distinction in the extent of teleworking between, on the one hand, most services, such as technological services, consultancy and public administration, which had an average of teleworking higher than the national average, and, on the other hand, the manufacturing industry, construction, or the services that we have come to call essential, such as retail, social and health services, or restaurants and hotels, all with shares of teleworking well below the average and that typically require a greater degree of physical presence. It is true that, because it was mandatory, this period was exceptional in its use of teleworking, but it was, for that reason, also indicative of the (current) limits of its use.

There is another, particularly significant, dimension of inequality, one that reflects the specific occupations of workers and the way in which these are strongly linked to their qualifications. While experts in the intellectual and scientific professions have the highest incidence, with 67% teleworking during the period of confinement, only 1% of unskilled workers were able to telework during that period. In other occupations, such as plant and machine operators, skilled workers in industry and construction, or workers in personal, security and sales services, only 5% or less were teleworking, while technicians and associate professionals, managers, and administrative staff had between 44% and 60% teleworking. This clear distinction between occupations (and, partially, qualifications) reflects a central inequality in the way different workers can, or cannot, access those benefits of autonomy in the management of time, space, and work itself, that teleworking provides, as well as in the impact that this autonomy can have on discipline and concentration at work or on the balance of professional and family life. It should also be added that, Jon Messenger's assertion to the contrary notwithstanding, during this period of confinement in the pandemic there was greater use of teleworking by women in Portugal. In part, this was certainly an effect of the distribution of occupations between men and women, the latter being more represented in those occupations more 'teleworkable', rather than a choice among couples on a distribution of responsibilities as regards looking after minors at home during this period. Despite this, it should be noted that many men (31%) were teleworking during this period, and so had a new experience of balancing work and family life throughout working hours.

3. The regulation of tensions in teleworking

One of the main impacts of teleworking identified in a number of international studies (e.g. Eurofound, 2020; Felstead, 2021), in the aforementioned study in Portugal, and emphasised by Messenger, is the fact that teleworkers typically work more hours than those working at the employer's premises, often extending into evening and weekend periods. Thus, in addition to the indirect costs associated with problems in negotiating the boundary between professional and family space, the benefits of teleworking have very concrete direct effects on the work relationship. Jon Messenger notes that a number of studies suggest that there are positive effects in terms of individual performance, motivation and even job satisfaction that result from the autonomy provided by teleworking, as well as in terms of the reduction of time spent travelling between home and work, but he also stresses the need to better understand these (im)balances. We are currently developing research precisely with the objective of analysing how different models of telework, specifically a hybrid regime that combines remote and face-to-face work, respond to these tensions.

Jon Messenger has some suggestions for the development of public policies in order to, on the one hand, enhance the benefits of teleworking and, on the other hand, mitigate the risks that arise in part from the aforementioned tensions. All of this became evident in Portugal during the pandemic, in particular the issue, not mentioned by Messenger, of the direct costs associated with working conditions at home, specifically the physical infrastructure, incurred by teleworkers. The public debate over these issues led to amendments of the Portuguese Labour Code in 2021 (cf. Law no. 83/2021, of 6 December) with a view to bringing about a more effective regulation of both the conditions of access to teleworking and the obligations of the parties. The new rules seek to ensure that telework can be an effective way to help reconcile professional and personal life, but also that it is an instrument that does not impose inequalities in relation to face-to-face work. Thus, the new legislation has extended the situations in which workers have the right to teleworking to include those who have children up to the age of eight or who have been recognised as informal caregivers. The law also clarifies the employer's financial obligations related to teleworking, protects teleworker's privacy in the face of hierarchical control issues, recognises the risks of isolation for the teleworker and seeks to guarantee situations of equality between workers and teleworkers in a number of matters, including collective representation. To an extent, these changes are in line with those recommended by Messenger. But Messenger's recommendations also reflect the ambiguity of the tensions affecting teleworking and the difficulty of regulating them. From the outset, the tension between autonomy in time management and the flexibility of working hours – something that impacts on work duration and enables its intrusion into personal and family life – is a central issue. It was in relation to this aspect, the so-called "right to disconnect," that the Portuguese legislator intervened also. The discussion of the recognition of a "right to disconnect" is a natural consequence of the situation described by Jon Messenger, and one that has seen important developments in recent years.

4. Teleworking and the "right to disconnect"

The "forced normalisation" of teleworking brought about by the COVID-19 pandemic lent greater visibility to the issue of what is known as "right to disconnect". According to Eurofound (2021), "the right to disconnect refers to a worker's right to be able to disengage from work and refrain from engaging in work-related electronic communications, such as emails or other messages, during non-work hours." With the increase in the number of teleworking workers, and the extension of this new order of working thanks to successive waves of the pandemic, the advantages of working wherever and whenever you want have given way to concerns about its risks and adverse effects. Subsequentlty, the problems of *overwork* and of the spatio-temporal uncertainty regarding work and non-work have become increasingly visible.

This discussion of the right to disconnect is rooted in the processes of technological innovation of recent decades, and did not arise only because of telecommuting. Increasing mobility in communications and electronic devices has made it possible, even for those who are not teleworkers, to shrink the distance between themselves and their employer. Availability to respond to company requests outside working hours and the place of work has become part of the ethos of many organisations and serves as a measure of the quality and commitment of individual employees. It also puts pressure on them.

Recently, some companies, mainly multinationals, have introduced into their strategies for digital transformation regulations aimed at limiting contact by email or cell phone with workers during their rest times. In 2012, Volkswagen decided to begin blocking the circulation of emails after working hours and, in 2016, the French company Orange, following negotiations with the unions, adopted a right to disconnect for its workers. In 2020 and 2021, respectively, the multinationals UniCredit Group and Solvay signed agreements with their European Works Councils (EWCs) that provided for rules and guidelines on this matter.

Such initiatives have not been confined to business. A growing number of EU countries have adopted regulation in this regard. In France the right to disconnect was enshrined in labour law in 2016. Subsequently, Italy, Spain, France, Belgium, Greece, Slovakia and Portugal have also legislated on this matter. Portuguese legislators opted for a general duty on employers not to keep employees constantly on call outside working hours, except in situations of *force majeure*, rather than a right of workers to disconnect (article 199-A of the Labour Code, amended by Law no. 83/2021, of 6 December). This general duty is especially reinforced in the case of teleworkers, as is clear from article 169-B, /1, *b*). Violation of this duty is considered to be a serious offence.

At the level of the EU, the European Parliament resolution of 21 January 2021 on the right to disconnect [2019/2181(INL)][119] should also be pointed out. In that resolution, MEPs recognised that "the right to disconnect is a fundamental right which is an inseparable part of the new working patterns in the new digital era" (Cons. H) and that it should be formally espoused because "constant connectivity combined with high job demands and the rising expectation that workers are reachable at any time can negatively affect workers' fundamental rights, their work-life balance, and their physical and

---

[119] See Official Journal of the European Union C 456/161, of 10.11.202, in https://eur-lex.europa.eu/legal-content/EN/TXT/PDF/?uri=CELEX:52021IP0021&from=EN

mental health and well-being" (Cons. J.2), particularly in the case of "the most vulnerable workers and those with caring responsibilities" (Cons. H). In this resolution, the European Parliament urges the Commission to propose a directive enshrining the fundamental right to disconnect, while calling on Member States to create conditions, specifically through collective bargaining, that allow workers to exercise this right without fear of retaliation or discriminatory treatment by employers.

The trend of regulation in the EU seems to favour hard law solutions, through the enshrining of a fundamental right of workers or the imposition of a duty on employers. Ireland took the path of soft law, when, in 2021, the Workplace Relations Commission (WRC) approved a code of conduct for all workers and employers, whether teleworking or not, that contained principles on the obligation not to keep workers constantly on call and the right to disconnect. The WRC's aim is to establish, whether in collective or individual bargaining, a policy on the right to disconnect that effectively balances the interests of companies and the needs of their workforce.

5. Final Note

The spatial and temporal autonomy that technologies provide to work relations brings with it, as Messenger emphasises, "both new opportunities and new challenges". While the opportunities are usually quickly identified and taken advantage of, the challenges can be more difficult to recognise and address. This asymmetry cannot be allowed to serve as an obstacle to robust regulatory action that establishes minimum legal standards of protection for telecommuting workers, standards that can subsequently be improved and reinforced in the context of collective bargaining.

It is true that the problems raised by teleworking most immediately affect those more qualified workers who benefit most from teleworking. However, the increasing centrality of ICT in the world of work – consider for example "platform work"[120] – indicates that the challenges and risks of digitalisation must quickly become the subject of public discussion and regulation, particularly when they affect those workers who are more vulnerable than most teleworkers.

References:

Eurofound (2021), *Right to disconnect – Definition*. In: https://www.eurofound. europa.eu/observatories/eurwork/industrial-relations-dictionary/right-to-disconnect.

Eurofound (2020), 'Living, Working and COVID-19', Publications of the European Union, Luxembourg.

Felstead, A and Reuschke, D (2020) 'Homeworking in the UK: before and during the 2020 lockdown', *WISERD Report*, Cardiff: Wales Institute of Social and Economic Research.

Pereira, T.S.; Silva, A.A.; Pires, E.; Lamelas, F.; Reis, J.B.; Manso, L.; Estêvão, P.; Carvalho, T.M. (2021), 'Trabalho, Teletrabalho e Distanciamento Social em situação de Pandemia', Relatório Final Projeto 804 Concurso FCT RESEARCH4COVID-19, CoLABOR – Laboratório Colaborativo para o Trabalho, Emprego e Proteção Social.

---

[120] See the Proposal for a Directive of the European Parliament and of the Council on improving working conditions in platform work, of 9.12.2021 [COM(2021) 762 final], in https://eur-lex.europa.eu/legal-content/EN/TXT/PDF/?uri=CELEX:52021P C0762&from=EN

FINAL REMARKS
THE ILO CHAIR AND THE FUTURE OF WORK

Manuel Carvalho da Silva[121]

In 2016, I had the privilege of being part of the team that worked on the International Labour Conference Simulation. In the aftermath, in the following year, I was very pleased to learn that the Faculty of Economics of the University of Coimbra (FEUC) had created the "ILO Chair". The ILO's key themes favour the sharing of the kinds of knowledge that cut across a university's multiple areas of teaching and research.

However, in the overwhelming majority of Portuguese universities, notably in such prime areas as sociology, law, economics and engineering, the study of work (and of trade unionism and employers' organisations), which needs to be thorough and sustained, has played a secondary role and the study of the organisation of work has basically been handed over to finance-driven approaches to management. This neoliberal option has become a determining factor in shaping the country's economy and its development. Therefore, FEUC should be commended for creating this forward-looking Chair.

My high expectations have been confirmed by the contents of the Chair's first three seminars, which were held between 2018 and

---

[121] University of Coimbra, Centre for Social Studies and CoLABOR - Collaborative Laboratory for Labour, Employment and Social Protection.

https://doi.org/10.14195/978-989-26-2277-4_17

2020 and are now being brought to a wider audience. Put together and imaginatively designed by Professor Hermes Augusto Costa, the present volume provides the space for a "conversation" in which a group of academics from various backgrounds – all familiar with the ILO – respond to the contents of seminars given by a number of highly qualified ILO cadres. Based on studies or research carried out by the academics in their own fields, these responses make the conversation richer and widen its scope.

By way of concluding the volume, I too propose to enter into conversation with the contents of its eight chapters, albeit without embarking on an analysis of the contents of each of them individually. Given that only one of these first three sessions took place in the context of the COVID-19 pandemic, mine will be a somewhat generic approach. Future volumes will no doubt address the broader "devastating effects on the world of work" arising from the impacts of the pandemic, as well as the way in which the latter was managed at the global, regional and State level.

I wish to begin by highlighting the fact that, in June last year, the ILO adopted a "global call to action for a human-centred recovery from the COVID-19 crisis that is inclusive, sustainable and resilient" (ILO, 2021). In terms of the analysis and proposals contained in it, this was an extremely timely and relevant gesture on the part of the ILO. In fact, the call to action showed that the pandemic has shed an even harsher light on problems that were already known and that the "crisis has exacerbated pre-existing decent work deficits, increased poverty, widened inequalities and exposed digital gaps within and among countries." (p.1)

Although during the initial stages it was often said that the COVID-19 pandemic "affected everyone equally", the ensuing crisis "disproportionately affected the disadvantaged and the vulnerable". This means that the time has come to seek answers to problems that lie even deeper in a number of fields and in various echelons of the world of work, notably as far as the evolution of work and employment patterns is concerned. In this regard, let me say that we should not confuse new ways of organising and performing work with new types of employment and that it is imperative that we take climate and environmental challenges very seriously, taking into consideration what is known as the double (i.e., environmental and digital) transition and other ongoing transitions.

The Simulation carried out at the University of Coimbra in the academic year 2016/2017 had shown that, if correctly presented, the complex issues related to work both at present and in the future, as well as the rights and obligations entailed, remain a concern for young people and make them enthusiastic participants in the debate. Hence the participation, in both the preparatory and in the more formal sessions of the Simulation, of hundreds of students from various levels and areas.

It is not only necessary, but also perfectly feasible, to generate the confidence and the motivation that lead the young to action. The effects of technological and scientific advances do not have to be apocalyptic, as is often depicted in conjectural scenarios in the area of the future of the economy, work, employment, and the organisation of society. Quite the contrary. If we train the young so that they develop a confident, responsible and proactive attitude vis-à-vis the potential effects of technological and scientific advances and train them to be rigorous in the study of the many implications of those advances, the new generations will certainly be in a better position to take all available technology and all existing knowledge, as well as the entire potential of the tools of work, and put them at the service of humans, the safeguarding of the environment, and life on the planet.

All of us, and young people in particular, are increasingly aware of the fact that the digital age, robotisation and artificial intelligence is also the age of environmental and ecological dilemmas, of heated confrontations between democracy and authoritarianism, of the pressing need to design better public policies, of profound and irrational inequalities, of increased life expectancy and novel demographic dynamics and of a major investment in lifelong training and skilling. Furthermore, it is the age of the commodification of work, notwithstanding the fact that "labour is not a commodity to be traded in markets for the lowest price" (ILO, 2019: 38).

The factors currently influencing the new social and universal division of labour are legion, the most salient of them being those that stem from the geopolitical and geostrategic changes now underway. Not infrequently, the tectonic shifts observed both in the established and the new powers are the ones making the strongest impact in terms of creating the conditions for the structuring and organisation of the economy or societies across a wide range of fields.

If, as Pope Francis argued in his address to the 2021 ILO Conference, it is vital – and it certainly is – that we enter a new (or renewed) Social Contract if we are to navigate the future with confidence, it is all the more imperative that we analyse and take on the challenges listed above in all their ramifications. It would therefore be dishonest, for example, to address the entire framework of labour and social rights based on alleged technological determinisms, or to view those rights as market impositions and a product of the goals of the financialised economy.

The financialisation of the economy has greatly blurred and eroded the value of work, the role of wages and of basic work rights, and the relationship between individual and collective rights. It has also mounted a structural assault on Labour Law, which came to be viewed as a tool of business management put at the service of "competitiveness", thereby denying its own specific genesis and mission. At the same time, these profoundly neoliberal tendencies in the economy allow employers and business actors in general to hide and escape accountability (at least until now) in the systems of employment relations. We are thus faced with a perilous subversion.

The tripartite foundation of the slow but steady affirmation of decent work consisted of the following elements: freedom of organisation and collective representation – of workers, to begin with, but of employers as well; the establishment and affirmation of Labour Law as a specific branch of Law, the primary mission of which is to protect the weaker party; true collective bargaining as the single most relevant factor in terms of the distribution of wealth and the fostering of equality in the second half of the 20th century. No new Social Contract will ever be made possible by tearing down these mechanisms and adopting the logic of wealth accumulation, a wealth that is generated by labour for the benefit of a few and through the imposition of rampant individualism.

As argued in the Report alluded to, it is imperative that we harness change – which is vast and comes from many fields –, not in order to exclude or isolate citizens, but to promote full integration into society, to create jobs, and to value work. The report further states that "countless opportunities lie ahead to improve the quality of working lives" and that we need to "seize the moment to reinvigorate the social contract" and use a "human-centred agenda" (OIT, 2019: 10) in order to address the new forces that are transforming work (OIT, 2019: 44). New technologies can no doubt be applied either by focusing on "the machine" to the detriment of the characteristics and conditions of human beings/workers or by putting human beings/workers centre stage while making sure that the technologies are rendered profitable. The latter hypothesis is the right path.

In most debates on the effects of technological innovation, the emphasis tends to fall on "the number of jobs that will be destroyed", the "occupations that are bound to disappear", and how the use of machines is not consistent with labour rights. The positives tend to go unmentioned or to be downplayed, despite the potential for creating new jobs, the lightening of the burden of work as a result of the redesigning of many occupations and professions, and the fact that the future is likely to bring a great variety of interesting and valuable professions and occupations.

The remarkable advances that have been achieved and the strides still waiting to be made have not robbed work of its centrality. In fact, they drive us to demand actively that work be creative, motivating and conducive to self-fulfilment, a universal right that generates individual and collective responsibility and helps create the conditions that permit the existence of organised, functioning societies.

I completely agree with the notion that the 1919 "constitution of the ILO remains the most ambitious global social contract in history" (OIT, 2019: 23). The ILO's founding principles – which make it clear that rights at work and the dignity of workers are structuring elements of social justice and peace –, its tripartite commitment, its programmatic bases and the conventions and recommendations it produced over the years have led to important achievements in terms of reducing working hours, combating exploitative forms of child and women's labour, and promoting basic labour rights. The Conference held by the ILO in Philadelphia in 1944 was a highly significant contribution to the Universal Declaration of Human Rights and to the very structure of the United Nations. A few decades later, the ILO formulated and affirmed its Decent Work Agenda.

The first part of the present book provides ample confirmation of how rich the historical legacy of this great universal institution is. In these times in which the exploitation and suffering of many millions of workers and their families is being made worse by the effects of the pandemic and the consequences of wars – now also in Europe –, the ILO's voice and interventions have become indispensable to avoid greater calamities.

It is imperative that we view and address work and its future role in political, social, economic and legal terms, in order to ensure that individual and collective rights, in addition to income and security, are guaranteed. Despite its limitations, the tripartite culture underlying the overall functioning of the ILO is the one best equipped to assume this broad outlook in a reformist and transformative way. Globally speaking, no other organisation is more bent on seeking integrated solutions of a socio-economic nature.

The ILO tells us that we can and must ensure that every single worker is covered by systems of social security and social protection, which in turn should be expected to be universal and based on solidarity. Individualism, together with the fragmentation of society and with the diminishing role, even annihilation of institutions and of the instruments of intermediation, conspire to block the construction of collective identities, muddle the organisation and role of collective labour relations, and erode the systems of social security and social protection. This means that the vitalisation and strengthening of labour institutions, of trade unions and employers' associations, and of collective bargaining and social dialogue are pressing needs. Although all this is fully acknowledged and accepted by the ILO, we are very far from a political dynamics in which such interpretations are acted upon.

When discussing the real implications for work that result from the digital switchover, robotisation, artificial intelligence, and all the transitions with which we are currently dealing, we must bear in mind that the fundamental rights of work are human rights. Let me transcribe two of the articles of the Universal Declaration, and simply allow them to speak for themselves:

Article 23 – 1. Everyone has the right to work, to free choice of employment, to just and favourable conditions of work and to protection against unemployment. 2. Everyone, without any discrimination, has the right to equal pay for equal work. 3. Everyone who works has the right to just and favourable remuneration ensuring for himself and his family an existence worthy of human dignity, and supplemented, if necessary, by other means of social protection. 4. Everyone has the right to form and to join trade unions for the protection of his interests.

Article 24 – Everyone has the right to rest and leisure, including reasonable limitation of working hours and periodic holidays with pay.

Workers' sovereignty over their own time needs to be expanded. Time and health are the two major pillars of life. Let us not forget that, unlike machines, human beings need to distinguish between working time and non-working time, and to respect the distinction between day and night. Let us take these key issues and the entire Decent Work Agenda and make them part of our debates, our research and our actions.

Even if machines are becoming "smart", the social relationships and the intermediations that we need will continue happen between and among human beings.

References

Organização Internacional do Trabalho (2019), *Trabalhar para um futuro melhor* (Comissão Mundial sobre o Futuro do Trabalho). Lisboa: OIT.

Organização Internacional do Trabalho (2021), *Apelo mundial à ação para uma recuperação da crise da COVID-19 centrada nas pessoas que seja inclusiva, sustentável e resiliente* (Resolução adotada na Conferência Internacional do Trabalho). Genebra: OIT.